52 Churches

Steven Charles

ISBN 0-7414-4696-0

www.52CHURCHES.com

Published by:

INFINITY
PUBLISHING.COM

1094 New DeHaven Street, Suite 100
West Conshohocken, PA 19428-2713
Info@buybooksontheweb.com
www.buybooksontheweb.com
Toll-free (877) BUY BOOK
Local Phone (610) 941-9999
Fax (610) 941-9959

Printed in the United States of America

Printed on Recycled Paper

Published September 2008

PREFACE

This book is designed as an "easy read" and was primarily written for alcoholics and drug addicts. Secondly, it is written for the families, relatives and friends of alcoholics and drug addicts. It is a view of religion but it also has political ideas designed to get everyone thinking and working together in order to find solutions to the problems that face all of us.

Unlike a good meal, a good book will still be there when you are finished with it. For that reason, and since this book was written for several different types of people, I would like for you to keep a list (*while you are reading*) of anyone that you could loan your copy to when you are finished.

I recommend that you read one church/chapter each morning so you'll have time to completely process what I've said. Somewhere in the book there may be parts that you don't agree with, and I will gladly accept your input. But as you continue reading, please remember the main goal of this book and the process that I have listed above. It might also be helpful for all of us to read this book several times. I hope you, your family, and your friends continue to enjoy the investment you made in this book.

Sincerely,

Steven Charles

INTRODUCTION

I just got out of prison!!! I wish I could bottle up this feeling and give it to all of the sad or spoiled people in the world because I know there are a lot of people who could use new starts in their lives. They need new starts because their lives got off track and mixed up from the way they lived or the way they are living right now. I hope some of you can gèt your new start without having to go to prison first, like I did.

Getting out of prison is a real rush! It is almost overwhelming. I'm lucky enough to still have my mom and she picked me up when they finally opened the gates and let me out. Our first stop was a perfect freedom flash when she whipped in the drive-thru at McDonald's. We didn't plan it, but it was a taste of freedom I can't begin to describe to you. Unless you have been locked up, there is no way to describe what real food tastes like after being "gone" for a few years!

I wanted to start this book immediately upon my release and I did. I wanted to spend my first year back in the free world with you so you can experience all the emotions and thoughts of an alcoholic/addict as he returns to the "free world." Writing this will help me and I also hope it will help others. It might even help you help someone who has a problem with their life that they themselves cannot see.

I am writing this book in hopes of keeping people from wasting their lives worshipping alcohol and drugs like I did for so long. Living with high self-esteem without drugs will lead us to true happiness which I think is everyone's goal in life. Happiness or contentment, God or your Higher Power, whatever your religious outlook, the fact is we all live on one planet and it all boils down to the fact that most of us should have the same objectives. Hopefully this book will help us understand how to live and enjoy all of the things that many of us take for granted.

Ch 1

My first Church/Chapter is at my mom's church and takes place on a perfect Easter Sunday. I guess it's my church also now since I stuck to my prison plan and got baptized there. My baptism was one of the first things on my "to do" list. It was very special for me and a little six-year-old girl got baptized too. By doing this I am sticking to my decision to make every effort possible to stay out of that miserable place they call prison. As far as I'm concerned prison is one of the many "hells on Earth" although there are many places worse than an American prison. I hope this action of faith will help me when I'm faced with my demons (alcohol, speed, weed, sex, etc.). My baptism lets you know that this first stop in my book is a Christian church.

One part of the service was Communion where they give you a piece of bread and some grape drink. This church has communion every Sunday. Communion is the partaking of the consecrated bread and wine. This represents the body and blood of Christ. This church uses grape juice, some use water, and some use real wine.

Well, good morning! It's now Wednesday and I'm up early for my first rain storm in the "free world!" It felt great to be able to stop and watch the rain or go back inside whenever you want, but the rain is almost over and it's going to be a beautiful sunrise. I'M FREE and so happy!

If you don't think today is a good day just try missing one by being locked up. It's hard for some people to understand how excited an ex-con can get at little things that most people take for granted. I saw a new $10 bill and I was shocked at how different the new design looked. Everybody looked at me funny. They probably figured out that I had been locked up for a while or maybe they thought I was from another country. I felt like I was from another planet! When you get out and first begin riding in a car again, you feel like a little kid taking their first trip to New York City! Everywhere you go, you are looking at all the stores, and the restaurants, and everything else. It really feels great!

I wrote some of the guys back at the unit as soon as I got home and have already received some letters back. Getting mail in "the joint" is a really big deal. Most people are forgotten once they end up behind bars. Now they are of no use to the "users" that they used to call friends. The best thing for me when I write back to prison, is remembering what it was like being incarcerated and how easy it would be to go back. We all need to focus on how lucky we are to be free.

Sometimes we wonder what the meaning of life is and we wonder why we should even make an effort. We see all the major problems in the world and it can cause us to lose our faith or hope for the future. We may see others doing great things and we may think that they can take care of everything and that they don't need me or us. We could work hard toward something, but then one day everything will all be over anyway, so why should we even try. Well there are several good reasons so let's cover a few of them.

Your life is yours and no one else's. So what you do with it is mostly up to you. You can waste it but it's not like you'll get another chance someday. You only get one shot on this Earth so why not enjoy it. You could party away your life and that would be fine if it made you happy. You could party away your life and that would be fine if it didn't make you feel so bad. You could party away your life and that would be fine if it didn't end up ruining your life and perhaps the lives of others. You could party away your life if it didn't make the ones who love you cry. You will not know what you are doing is wrong until you learn and believe what you are doing is wrong. Everyone needs to feel they have some value even if it's only to themselves. Finding any kind of job will start this process and then a “slow and steady” approach will lead you to better jobs and better situations.

But work alone may not be enough. You may need the support of others—Church, Recovery Groups, etc. You may need to join some kind of club or group that benefits society—some group that doesn’t care about your social status or how much money you make. This type of personal progress, along with the loving care and appreciation of your simple belongings, will give you the satisfaction you need to stay sober and/or happy, depending on your own personal demons.

Once again, remember that alcohol, and especially other drugs, will destroy everything we have just discussed. We need to focus on this daily by reading positive mental-reinforcing material, by saying positive statements and/or praying. By doing this we can begin to eliminate some of our problems. Some of us may slip, but if we don’t give up and we continue to try harder each time, eventually we can beat all the problems that try to ruin our lives.

Taking care of yourself physically must be one of your top priorities. Without your physical well-being none of this will be possible. Taking care of your body will give you the mental energy you need so you can work toward other things that you would rather be doing. Walking is the easiest way to get started on an exercise program and water is the most important part of your diet. How you fuel your brain is very important too. After a good night’s sleep, your morning meal is very important. Eating breakfast sets your metabolism so it can burn calories during the day. Without this active metabolism, calories aren’t burned so they’re stored as fat. Instead of sugary foods or maybe even coffee, start your day with some fresh fruit for long-lasting energy. Then let that digest by itself for 45 minutes. Then you can have a small amount of protein. Today I started my day with eight ounces of water and then one cup of coffee while I read a couple of pages out of the Bible. I don’t have any fresh fruit yet so I ate one egg and one slice of bacon. Then I exercised for about 20 minutes and took a shower. Then I meditated and/or cleared my mind—focusing on my main objective for the day.

Don't let your life-style habits hold you in bondage. Learn from the past, live for the moment, work for the future! And remember, your day will be just like your attitude so let your face shine.

Start your new life today, I am!

Ch 2

This week I decided to go to a church on Saturday so that on Sunday, I could go back to the church where I was baptized. I didn't want to just "disappear" right after I was baptized and I needed to see what the Saturday Sabbath was all about anyway.

It was a real nice place with some very, very good singers. They had a wonderful big screen so we could sing along which was much easier than looking at the songs in a book. My eyes are starting to get bad so I really liked that. But the solo vocals were some of the best singers I have ever heard! They were as good as any professionals I've ever heard! The guy running the sound board had long hair and I could picture him "back in the day" working for a rock band. He had his Harley parked outside and maybe someday I'll ride my bike back for a visit.

There were lots of kids, and they all were very well behaved. They stayed for the main service and were very involved with the whole program. At one point they sat on the steps of the stage and talked about their favorite stories in the Bible. After the regular collection plate went around, it was time for the "lamb" collection. That's what they called it when all of the kids had little buckets and came around for metal money. It was a happy time when the sound of the money jingled as they smiled and ran around the room.

This church believes that the Old and New Testaments were written by inspiration from God who has infinite wisdom and unyielding love for all of us, and that Jesus is God's son and he is our only way to salvation and eternal life. I think we all still wonder what type of eternal life that will be. These Christians also believe that Jesus lived on Earth in divine nature. He lived a life we should all try to follow. He died to pay for the sins we have all made and then he returned to His Father on our behalf. They believe that the Holy Spirit is the regenerating power that provides our strength to accomplish all of the things in life that we need. To obtain your salvation, you must transform your life and your way of thinking about life, by what they call a "new birth." This ordinance of the Christian Church is finalized with the baptism by immersion. The Ten Commandments are by far the most important laws of any and the fourth commandment sets the Sabbath day as the seventh day of the week which is our Saturday. The Sabbath is a day of rest where your soul can purge itself of less important details and prepare for the following week.

Today is Earth Day and the members of this church really respect the Earth. Each month they have a special recycling drive. Everyone gets their neighbors to save aluminum, plastic, glass and paper which they then get together and combine for the recycle center. All of the clean paper is easy to separate and send to the recyclers—newspapers, magazines, phone books, junk mail, and even opened envelopes. All you need is a separate trash can for them. The other items are more important because of how long they last. Plastic water bottles are real easy to save but the other drink containers need to be rinsed out. Electronics are one of the most important items that have been added to recycling programs. One of the top computer makers said they will take your old computer equipment when you buy a new one. Hopefully they will dispose of them properly but there are some people who care more about making money than they do about the environment. I saw on television where huge machines chew up old electronics and separate and save the materials they were made from. But it's still cheaper to dispose of old electronics in developing nations. Over half of the world's electronic waste is shipped to China where the poor people dismantle it with no regard for the health risks. Washington State leads our nation by recycling 42% of their solid waste and our national average is 27%. If you care about your planet, look under "recycling" on the internet and start doing your part, and help your neighbors and friends do their part also. Our kids and their kids will be very glad we did.

Ch 3

This week I went to a mostly "black" church, and since I am "white," it was another new church experience for me. They had a great choir and a real set of drums, which I had never seen at a church before! They really put on a great show with a lot of singing and fancy hand-waving praise dancing. One girl in particular was so pretty that I had to keep reminding myself that I was in a church—but I have been locked up for a while! This church had "Saint" in their name so I was curious about that, and it also had "missionary" in their name. When I think of Saints, I think of Catholics but this wasn't a Catholic church. In Latin saint would be *Sanctus* and would translate as "holy". A saint's soul would be in heaven. A saint would be anybody who was deemed worthy by a large group because they were a great yet humble leader and were involved in many charitable works. They would have very closely followed the traits that Jesus asked all of us to follow. Missionary, or *missio* in Latin, means "sending". Most missions are for spreading Biblical faiths. A Greek person sending a message would be an *apostle*. Missionaries are people who travel to spread a religious message.

The word missionary made me think of many people. One was Adoniram Judson who lived from August 9, 1788 to April 12, 1850. He was a very bright child who mastered everything he studied including reading from the Bible at three years old. As a young man he went to college where he rebelled from his parents' teachings. He was smart and he loved having people listen to him. He dreamed of being a great leader in this country. However later in life he was bothered by the questions he couldn't find answers to. The same questions many wise men have wondered about—like life after death, etc. He decided that Christianity made the most sense out of the unexplainable. He stopped his efforts towards fortune and fame, and he decided to take his idea of Christianity to Rangoon, Burma. And like this week's church, his religion was based on Baptist teachings.

On the way to Burma, his wife Ann had a child. But the conditions on the ship were so bad that the baby died. Many religions and churches "compete" for followers and in Burma he had to compete mostly with Buddhism. Missionaries, definitely including Adoniram and Ann Judson, endured horrible sufferings in their quest to bring their message to distant lands. To do this Adoniram had to change from speaking the English language to speaking Burmese. He was so dedicated that he translated the whole Bible into Burmese. He was there six years before he found and taught a faithful follower. In the Karen jungles it is estimated that they saved/brought 20,000 people to the Christian faith. At one point he was put into a horrible prison. It wasn't even fit for animals and he was also tortured. Like most prisoners, after a while even Ann stopped visiting him. Then finally they let Adoniram go and by the time he found his wife, she was barely alive. However, they reclaimed their lives and continued teaching. Then after 14 years she died. Thirty-eight years later, there were over 200,000 Christians in the area.

I never thought getting high was that bad. I always considered myself "just a minnow in a sea of crime!" But Adoniram's trip across the sea must have been a scary adventure and you must really believe in something to put yourself at such risk. They believed that God created the Earth and the oceans and whatever happened to them was God's will. As special as the land is, the ocean has much more to teach us. Isn't it interesting how the ocean was designed with salt but at the same time, He designed other stuff that won't grow in salt water. Even more interesting is that the planet Earth is about two-thirds water and our bodies are about two-thirds water and the oceans and our bodies both have salt in them. The water that's classified as "ocean" covers 139 million square miles with an average depth of around 12,000 feet with half of it being over 9,000 feet deep. You can keep your mind happy by studying the oceans, and most of the life in it is found around 650 feet where there is still some sunlight. Where there aren't any land continents, the Earth's crust is covered with solidified volcanic rock called Basalt which comes mostly from the Earth's hot core. God, or whatever you want to call whoever created us and this magical place we live on, must have really been smart because the estimated odds of it happening by accident are 10^{65} to 1. That's a one followed by 65 zeros which means it would be almost impossible for it to have just happened by accident.

Staying off drugs is smart and you can do this by keeping your mind busy. If you get spoiled and lazy, you'll forget how fortunate you are to be able to do all of the things that you do on a daily basis. Even if you're not on drugs, take a break, relax and sit with your eyes closed for a minute. Now pretend that this "nothing" is all that you have (sort of like prison). If you are happier with your eyes closed, then you need to get rid of some stuff. Otherwise, WAKE UP and be amazed at all there is in front of you!

Ch 4

This week I went to one of the Methodist churches in our neighborhood. It was in a building that used to be an old grocery store but they had really fixed it up nice and made it into a place where the whole neighborhood could come and meet. It had a "court" but not like the ones that I've been used to going to. Theirs was the COURT OF PRAISE. This church had a lot of young people and some girls danced a little routine they had worked up to go along with the music. It was really cute! They also had two big screens with beautiful pictures projected behind the words of the songs we were singing. The band had professional type equipment, even a set of Pearl drums. The pastor was fairly young and the sermon was about relationships, he even dared to mention sex. I wish I could go back next week but I'll have to continue my journey. He talked a little bit about what they would be covering and it seemed to focus on waiting until you're married to have sex or at least staying with just one person. He said it was important to respect yourself or you won't be able to respect others or appreciate things the way God intended us to. When you care enough about your body to take care of it, you are appreciating nature and everything God designed. After you learn to take care of yourself, then you can learn to take care of this planet that God must have designed for us. It is a very complicated planet and deserves some respect. There are so many interesting things you can focus on when you are bored besides drugs or alcohol—like many of us did and some still do. Doing drugs or drinking alcohol usually results from being too lazy to look for other ways to entertain yourself. *Fun is short-lived, but true happiness is eternal!*

Nature and the environment are in trouble because many of us run around searching for ways to have fun. We live "the good life" and we don't like to walk anywhere or get too hot or too cold so we burn electricity, and we just lay around getting fat. We also like to stay up late at night with the lights and television on and do all sorts of things that burn electricity. Scientists worldwide are telling us that the surface of our planet is getting warm enough that it could start to cause us a lot of trouble. This global warming trend causes climate change and doesn't mean that your weather will be warmer. You may experience much colder weather depending on where you live.

Our oceans have acted like a carbon filter for decades but it's only a matter of time before they absorb too much. The oceans have about 50 times more carbon in them than our atmosphere does and sometimes this gets released back into the air. Over the last century the carbon dioxide in our atmosphere stayed around 280 PPM (parts per million) until around 1900 when it began to spike up drastically and at last count it was at about 380 PPM. The average world temperature was 57° but now the average is up to 58°. One degree can be the difference between ice or ice becoming water. Then if our oceans get too warm the Phytoplankton dies. This reduces the food all marine life needs to start the feeding process which leads to much of the world's food supply. Northern ice caps are melting earlier each year. If the sea level rises a few inches, many areas will be flooded with salt water. The salt in the water will kill the crops that farmers depend on to make a living, and crops that the rest of us depend on to provide us with nice meals. Many areas will flood but some will get severe droughts. The droughts not only kill animals and crops but they allow large fires to start which destroy neighborhoods. If the trend continues, many people in the world will have to move closer together because of the negative changes that will occur to what was once a balanced natural cycle. Farmers will have to adjust to different growing seasons and grow different crops. To keep animals alive, ranchers may have to pipe water across the country like oil is piped now. Removing the salt from the sea water will become big business and it may become the only alternative to rainfall in some areas. Purifying 300,000 gallons of "fresh" water costs about $200 compared to sea water at $650. Some businesses only see "dollar signs" as the frozen sea melts and they take advantage of the new areas for shipping, drilling and mining.

Over the last 200 years, man has changed the Earth faster than he has ever before. It's hard to believe that the smartest mammal of our time avoids thinking about the future. Environmentalists have many suggestions so that everyone can help, but we have to be willing to make adjustments. Hopefully we can learn ways to make adjustments that won't raise our electric and fuel bills. By the time this book is published, many ideas and problems mentioned in it may be old news and I hope we have solved some of our problems. One of the best and easiest ways to help with this problem is to replace your standard light bulbs with compact fluorescent light bulbs, but they are made with Mercury and need to be disposed of properly.

Cars that run off batteries and alternative fuels will help reduce our need for oil. But batteries can create more problems when they get old because they must be disposed of properly. Properly means the best way possible. Disposing of small batteries is something that most people don't do properly—they just throw them in with the rest of their trash. The toxic metals they are made of go back into our air and water when they sit at the local dump or when they are burned. Alternative fuels will create new challenges also. Ethanol is made mostly from corn, corn stalks, and sugar cane, but it can also be made from grass and wood. This will make corn more valuable and will raise the price of feed which will raise the price of beef, but at least the money could stay in our country and out of the Middle East. But when anything gets valuable some people will try to manipulate the process. Fertilizers are chemicals and if they are used to grow plants faster they could harm our rivers and oceans and do more harm than good. Biodiesel is made from vegetable oil, animal fat, and even algae which can run small engines or giant diesel engines that create electricity. Many people are turning to solar power for some or all of their electric needs. Different ways of using the sun's energy have been used for centuries and soon every rooftop will be solar. Some people are also using windmills. There are several styles of modern wind turbines. "Backyard" windmills are a $20-million-a-year industry and can cut household bills approximately 25%. Our oceans also have the capability to create enormous amounts of electricity with the natural currents and the constant movement of the waves.

The United States is responsible for over 20% of the world's "greenhouse gases." These are automobile exhaust fumes, other carbon dioxide gases, and a few other types of gases that create the blanket effect that holds in the Earth's heat—like a greenhouse does for growing plants. Most of this pollution comes from things that make our lives better like oil, coal, and natural gas. However it's not just Americans causing problems because Canada, Mexico, and countries far away from America are pumping out carbon dioxide gases and other pollutants too. America's driving habits need to change, but China will soon catch up to America's carbon emissions and I don't think the Chinese will give up this new found luxury which so many shoppers around the world have afforded them. Other countries' businesses, many of which are owned by Americans, operate with an economic advantage over the United States because some good Americans are concerned about our planet. Where do we draw the line on helping our planet and keeping jobs in this country? I do not know. But I do think since it is just one planet, everybody on it should play by the same rules.

Ch 5

It's Mother's Day so I went to church with mom again. So for my new church this week I remembered meeting some bikers who said they had a church that met at night so Friday we went and checked them out. Mom had heard the pastor play at a town festival and she said he was real good. He and his wife go to prisons to spread God's word and being an ex-inmate myself that was very interesting to me. I thought I would go back and talk to inmates when I got out. Maybe someday I will. I have to get this book written first.

It was a small church and when we walked in to the sanctuary he was playing a Jemi Hendrix tune! We found out later that he was showing the people who got there early what he had played at his recent visit to a local high school. He is about my age or a few years older and like me he survived the hard-partying seventies and eighties and a trip or two to prison. So when he preaches to people, he sounds real "down to earth." He sounds more like he is talking to a friend than someone who has the power of God vested in them and is telling you how you should be. But it was a rockin' good time and everybody boogied to his Christian rock jam. He has played with several big rock bands and he has a new CD coming out that has prisoners on the cover. I think I'll buy at least one!

All of this talk about prisons and prisoners brought back a lot of bad memories. First there's all of the waiting to go to court to find out how much of your life you're going to lose. That little bit of hope you kept for some miracle to happen is gone. You get your time and you succumb to the fact of going to "hell on Earth" yet you still have to wait in county jail for months before you can leave and get started on your years of punishment. Then one night they tell you to pack up and the next morning you get chained to another man and get on the chain bus that's either freezing cold or real hot. Your knees are crammed into the seat in front of you and if you decide you can't wait any longer to go to the bathroom, you have to take your "new friend" to the hole with you. After all day and many stops to pick up more poor suckers, you finally get to your prison and begin a new nightmare. They make you strip down naked and yell at you and when they finally give you something to wear, your next stop is to get your head shaved. They finally feed you, but then you have to sit and wait all day to get your housing assignment. You are actually happy when you finally get to your steel bunk. You march to the chow hall again and eat the same slop that you will eat a thousand times before you go home. You get back to your bunk and try to sleep but it's too noisy and either very hot or very cold.

About one percent of the people in America are locked up. In prison, hell is not a place far away or in the future, but it has become your sad reality. After years go by, you try to forget about the real world. Some of "your people" write you at first but that ends after a year or so. You have your assigned job or go to school and one day is just like the next. When you get some time to watch TV, it's not on the channel you like and you can't hear it anyway so you better be able to read fast and follow the closed captions. You have to line up every two hours and be counted and if you're sleeping, they wake you and ask for your number. You also have to wake up early if you want clean clothes. Most of the time I washed mine myself or paid someone to. And you better not be shy because you are almost never alone. You smell them and they smell you. You wish that you had never been born.

Ch 6

This Sunday I missed church because the weather here was so nice that it had to be a motorcycle-riding weekend. So for our church this week, I went to one of the churches in town that had a meeting on a week night for anyone who is interested in other religions and it was a special on Buddhism. My friend Ray Neal, who was once on Alcatraz, introduced me to Buddhism while we were together in another prison. He was one mean dude back in the day, but now he's the nicest guy you could ever meet. He said Buddhism turned his life around so I guess there is something to it. I know we all need something in life to give us hope and faith. Life is a test, and you can fail or pass.

The Dalai Lama is the acting spiritual leader for Buddhists worldwide. Like most religions, there can be many different types and certain beliefs can vary. So we will attempt to cover some of the basics. Siddhartha Gautama was born around 560 B.C. The letters "B.C." stands for "before Christ" was born. After Jesus was born we register time as A. D. for "Anno Domini" which is Latin for "Year of the Lord". Siddhartha was born around the area we now call Nepal. His father was a prince but his mother died when he was very young. Trying to make him happy, his father gave him everything available. They were part of the Hindu group that believed you couldn't talk to God and only a Brahman priest could talk to God. At age 25, Siddhartha left on a quest for the "meaning of life." The first time he saw a sick old man, he was shocked and was afraid of his future. He was very worried about how nothing is permanent. First he tried fasting in order to return to the basics of life. He learned from this but he was still worried about death. One day while he was meditating he fell into a trance. When he awoke he felt enlightened and his fear was gone. Buddha means the enlightened one. He said the fact of God or no God has nothing to do with our happiness on this planet. And he said, "Health is the greatest gift, Contentedness is the greatest of riches, and someone's Trust is the greatest quality to possess." I say, "If I explain it to you, you may not believe it. But if I guide you, you will figure it out".

Buddhists celebrate what they call the "Four Noble Truths." First is the fact that suffering is part of life so get over it. Second is that suffering can be lessened by wanting less. Third is to not get attached to others because this will only make you sad when they leave. The fourth one is basically how to achieve the first three. Your thoughts and efforts must be positive so that they only create good. Like in Hinduism, this will build up good karma. This "karma" determines what happens to you after you die.

Well maybe I have a bunch of this karma stuff built up! I never was mean or hateful, well not very often anyway. I always helped everyone. I wasn't married and I had a truck so everyone always called me when they needed a ride or needed something moved. I got several DWI's taking people home or going to pick up someone who needed a ride. I never would have gone to prison if I had not answered the phone, left to help people and gotten those DWI's. I still would have been able to get probation if I got in trouble. Plus if I had stayed in the "Big City," they would have given me probation for my small-time crimes. But don't get me wrong, after it's "all said and done," I am glad that it turned out the way it did. I now know how to enjoy life instead of not realizing how good I have it. And I could still have been locked up if the lawyers and the judges and the parole board had wanted me to.

I tried almost every type of dope when I was young. But after that I would just drink beer and smoke pot mainly. After the first trip to prison, I quit all of it. But I was single and bored and easy prey for dope-heads who needed a place to party. Then I fell in love with a cute young woman. I was trying to get her off of speed, but I ended up getting back on it. I used to hate cigarettes and needles. When I got out of prison the first time I couldn't smoke weed anymore so I started smoking cigarettes. Then we started smoking speed. I have done dope my entire life, well since I was a teenager, but I never felt like a drug addict until I got on the needle.

Alcoholics and drug addicts are "dying to live." You can put a lot of things in your body and survive, but that doesn't mean you should. Nicotine kills more people than any other drug and alcohol kills six times as many as all the rest. How far down does your life have to go before you decide to tunnel your way out? If drugs are your treasure, that's where your heart will be. You won't care about much else. People who have been "hurt" by alcohol and drugs hate them more than most people but remember, the "lost" need you to listen more than they need you to talk.

Ch 7

It's Memorial Day weekend! My first big "party" holiday in the free world. And my first Memorial Day weekend party in the free world without any drugs or even any alcohol. To celebrate, I decided to go to the city to one of the biggest churches around—a Baptist church with over 15,000 members! They say about 6,000 people attend their services each weekend. Now it will be 6,001 with at least one ex-convict. It still sounds weird saying *convict*. I don't feel like an ex-con or even a criminal at all. Heck I just liked to party and have fun!

For those who are lost in sin, following God is hard at first. People who drink and drug have made their own religion which they call "partying." Their only way of dealing with the fact that someday we all will die is to drown their feelings with alcohol and drugs and "live for the moment!" They can't even consider quitting because they would lose their "friends" and their purpose in life. They will never be happy because they will always need more and "everybody has it better than they do." They will try to confuse their mind by keeping it busy just trying to survive and too dizzy to worry about reality and the things that are good about their lives.

Today it will be fun jumping in my truck and rolling to the city even though I won't have a buzz like the old days. Wish me luck and I'll see you when I get back.

Now I'm back and it was much different from my first six churches. It reminded me of my old rock concert days. I was born in a big city in the fifties, grew up in the sixties, partied hard during the seventies, eighties and nineties, and I saw almost every famous rock-n-roll band that ever toured. At this church, there were so many people trying to park and shuffle into the huge buildings that it barely seemed worth the hassle. Conversations with strangers were much shorter than at the smaller churches, and I couldn't shake the feeling of being out of place. Each church that I visit during this first year out of prison will feel a little strange, but after prison everything feels strange. The churches I like the most, I will return to some day. The next time I visit any of these churches, it will be much different since, by then, I will have more confidence and be more established in society. This church will be even bigger by then since they are planning on spending millions of dollars on construction.

There is no conclusive evidence as to the origin of Memorial Day. At one time it was called Decoration Day to celebrate decorating the graves from the Civil War. I wonder what would have happened if another country had attacked us during the Civil War? Would we have quit fighting each other? Memorial Day celebrates America's soldiers and one of the saddest things about prison is the old guys who fought for our freedom and then lost their freedom because they drank alcohol and drove a vehicle. Most of them didn't have a wreck or cause any trouble. They just got pulled over for speeding or not coming to a complete stop or an expired inspection sticker, or they just looked wild or any number of harmless violations. They drank every day since they returned from the war and then one day they got pulled over and the legal system lets them down. DWI/DUI laws are made to punish people for what they *might* do—they *might* have a wreck and they *might* hurt someone. If we used a more common-sense approach to punishment instead of a one-size-fits-all legal system, we could afford to lock up more gang members and keep violent child molesters locked up longer. When America decides to quit glorifying crime and start putting violent people in especially bad prisons with no televisions or weight machines and no parole, then we might be able to print newspapers full of good news. Crimes that do not involve violence or injuries should be given fines instead of prison so we could afford to keep violent people off the streets.

Old people in prison costs society more than it benefits society. I hate to say we need more government, but without creating a new study group, maybe we could vote to have a more realistic parole board. Keep the dangerous ones and let the others out early. Which means parole officers will have to let their best people off parole early to keep the parole system from growing. There are plenty of harmless people in prison and many more very violent people on the streets. Unfortunately, some of the people in prison are the type we will need to help us survive when times in America get rough. Odds of a catastrophe occurring soon are great and very real. There are different degrees of bad, and not all of them deserve prison. I hope that all of the fun, aggressive people aren't locked up when we really need them!

Ch 8

Well this week I wanted to check out a church we pass by all the time. A lot of cars are there every Sunday and Wednesday. It has "Bible" in their name, and it made me curious as to how "holy roly" it might be.

It ended up being one of my favorite churches so far. It also had sort of a "country" quality to it and it was as down-to-earth and as comfortable as you could possibly want. The musicians played an acoustic guitar, a fiddle (violin), and an instrument I believe was a clavichord. Everyone was dressed casually and so was I. Later, when I told a man that I had been locked up, he told me the pastor had been locked up too. Young people who had just graduated high school were there, and the pastor had a special sermon on making the right choices.

Now that I'm out, before each meal and even before the prayer, I pause and contemplate on what it would be like if I was still in prison. It helps keep me "centered" and focused on what's important in life. In prison you wait and wait until it's finally time for everyone in your building to go for chow. Then you march over to the chow hall and eat as much of the slop as you can before they make you get up and go right back to where you were ten minutes earlier.

Some mornings I wake up still tired from working hard the day before to get caught up on all of the things that I got behind on while I was locked up. I quickly think about all the unfortunate souls who are still paying for their mistakes and I rise to enjoy the benefits freedom offers.

Each night when I'm ready to go to sleep, I turn off the television and enjoy the peace and quiet. In prison you never have darkness or quietness. There is always someone yelling at their "homeboy" or someone thinking they're a rap star. The lights are always on and every couple of hours they wake you for a "head count." Peace and quiet—and even darkness—are truly underrated events that most people take for granted. When you lose your freedom, everyday is painfully and monotonously the same. Free people have choices to make and one of the most important is to use their time wisely. Of all God's creations, man is the only one who's aware of time. It goes by way too fast during good times, and crawls by very slowly during bad times.

The news just said a guy was arrested for something so bad I eventually decided to take the story out of this book. Evil knows no end, which is why we shouldn't give it a beginning. It is very hard to live like Jesus Christ when our animal instincts say different. The "little evils" we do keep us from working as hard as we could toward solutions to many problems that plague our society. The number of laws in a nation represents the amount of evil that's present. It's easy for people to drink a beer or get high and pretend "it's someone else's problem" until it affects their lives. When you become that "someone else" it may be too late to make any changes. That is why we should focus everyday on being the best person we can be. We tend to turn into "our society." If we are not careful, we will be led by what others do. We might have been led by television shows or music videos. We need to separate acting from real life. Taking your regular life and daily activities for granted is a sure way to end up losing them.

The largest causes of death today come from life-style choices. Last century Americans died mostly from sickness and wars. Smoking, poor diet and inactivity will slowly kill you. Today more people die from choices made involving alcohol and drugs. Things people do while drunk or on drugs kill people faster. However, drugs are such a major part of our world that I don't think people should be locked up for that crime alone. Being ungrateful for the life God gave you is a sure way to find out about heaven and hell or prison and Jesus. Faith in Christ will give the mystery of life a happy ending.

Ch 9

This week I went to a very small church. There are so many churches around here that sometimes I wonder how they can justify staying open. Well after visiting this church, I learned that there are so many different kinds of people, there will always be someone who feels more comfortable with a particular church. There weren't very many people there today but the ones who were there were obviously very grateful for having their lives improved through their faith in Jesus Christ.

I think most of the people who were there live in the neighborhood because some of them walked to church. Neighborhood churches are good because kids and people with no transportation can walk to church. Plus they can be with people they can call on if they ever need help in a hurry.

This is one of those churches where the members raise their hands in the air and sing and praise Jesus. The preacher was Oriental which instantly had me wondering how he had become a Christian. After church he told me that there were a lot of Christians where he came from. He used to be a "con" man, and he said he would tell you anything in order to get your confidence and business. After he turned his life over to Jesus, he ran a halfway house for homeless people and drug addicts. But he said in his old country there weren't very many homeless people because family members take care of the poor and elderly—but there are just as many drug addicts as there are in America. Several countries have problems with drug addicts and I hope one day this book will get translated into several languages.

The "Vision Statement" of this church is to bring people to Jesus and develop within them a Christ-like maturity so that they will be beneficial to others and represent the Christian way of life. Like me, this pastor is also worried about the government and their interpretation of religious freedom. He says the Orthodox Church seeks to restrict the activities of some Christian groups. A book by the Ministry of Education on religious conduct in our schools calls evangelical Christians "sects" and "neo-cults."

The Victims of Communism Memorial Foundation wants us to remember who fought for the freedoms that most of us enjoy today. We should all remember that one-fifth of the world still lives under total government rule and that those people know the effects of an over-powerful government. There is a very fine line, which no one seems to be able to define, that provides rules to govern a country safely. These rules or laws should provide guidance while at the same time they should not antagonize certain groups and make them angry. Common sense should be able to dictate when it is more important to make everyone happy or when it is necessary to upset a few for the benefit of the majority. There are many examples of this happening. As we all know, you cannot make everyone happy. The sooner we find a way for the majority of society to vote on each issue that plagues us, the better off society will be. We cannot continue to allow certain things to happen even though the Bill of Rights or the Constitution may state otherwise. To provide these freedoms for everything that any American can dream up is ridiculous.

Our courts are imploding from trying to accommodate and enforce all the new laws required to specify the details on behaviors that most people would not have considered when our country was originally founded. For stupidity to win, it only takes one judge to make a ruling—one who's afraid of violating the original old rules our forefathers set up back when the things currently being voted on were unheard of!

LET THE PEOPLE SPEAK! Our government is out of control. It has grown so large that the head doesn't know what the tail is doing. Maybe all of us should vote on each and every law. For example, if we had a voting system where, if more than 25% of interested Americans vote in favor of something, that law would be voted on again by each state. Then if at least 50% of the state votes in favor of something, it would be made a state law or it would be dropped until the next vote. Eventually by doing this, some of the things people want to do, but which are controversial, would either be completely eliminated or be separated by states. This way different people would be able to live like they want and there would still be laws in place to protect the people which certain laws were designed to protect. This would also eliminate locking up people for doing things that some people think should be legal. So after "everyone" votes, if your way or choice doesn't win, you can either move to another state or wait a couple of years and vote again.

Many crimes carry sentences that are too long and some aren't long enough. While we are voting we could also select punishments for each different crime. Punishments that we think would be appropriate if someone is found guilty. These punishments could range from a small fine to life in prison. Some types of crimes will have a chance at parole and some won't. By the whole country deciding and setting these predetermined punishments, we could relieve our overcrowded courts. If you're found guilty, then you are locked up for the amount of time that the majority of American citizens have determined you deserve.

The electronics are available which could easily be used to perform this type of voting. There are biometric devices that examine fingerprints and digital photos which would be matched with your other existing records to eliminate identity problems and prevent double voting. This way there would be no question as to what Americans really want. We could start with a few laws to test the process and work out any problems, and if it works, expand it each year. Does anyone else besides me see how many problems this could solve?

Ch 10

Well it's Father's Day and I called my dad! I had planned on going to see him if I was out of prison by this Father's Day, but things don't always work out like you plan when all you have to do is sit around and make plans. While I was locked up, I dreamed up a lot of things to do and maybe one day I will get some of them done.

My step-dad taught me the sign-making business and my father purchased a computer, program and plotter for me so I could start my own sign business. Before my first trip to prison, my dad also helped me purchase a house that's right on the highway with a shop so I can build sign frames. Since I've been out, I've been lucky enough to earn some money with my profession of sign-making. But the real work has come from the two houses and the seven acres mom and I are taking care of.

I am still waiting to find out if I'm a father or not with the help of the wild young woman I was with before my life was redirected by the State. Now, she's also on a State mandated vacation which is the best thing that could ever have happened to her. It's the only way she will get off, and have a chance to stay off, THE SPEED!

When I was young, the girls I dated were more interested in partying than raising a family. I guess I was too but I always thought that I would have been a good dad. Abortion was the new fad and I guess it must still be very popular since unmarried sex is rampant. I will give the "youngster," as I call her, credit for keeping her kids. She already had a four-year-old daughter when I hooked up with her but the drugs kept her from actually being a mother.

I thought I was too old to be a father but maybe not, only a test will tell. However I have helped raise several kids. On my way to get out of prison, I ran into a guy who lived with me about ten years ago. He helped me put up signs and we raised his two daughters for a couple of years. When I saw him for the first time in several years, we were in a county jail. I was in transit on the way to court to clear up another charge, and he was on his way to get started on his State time. And like most of us, he thought his parole was "right around the corner." Now it doesn't look like he'll be out before this book is out. He wrote me and wanted me to get him a Cowboy Bible, so I did and they also sent one to me.

So today, I grabbed my "Cowboy" Bible and traveled out into the country, or should I say farther out into the country, to a church with Cowboy in their name. I wore my cowboy boots, even though I'm no cowboy, but I do love my 4x4 truck. This church was in a barn and it was a little warm since it is summertime—but that gave it a real relaxed setting. They had a cross made out of horseshoes and sawdust on the floor. They had free coffee and doughnuts and we sat on wooden bleachers. There were lots of kids and grandparents and I think I was the only single person there. The kids were very well behaved and as soon as they got home they probably went horseback riding.

Their preacher talked about taking time for your kids, and slowing down and enjoying life which is now my main focus after prison. I go to church twice a week. I see parole twice a month. I stay with my mom as much as possible and I work on this book in my spare time. I hope you're enjoying it so far.

~Ch 11~

I had been reading a newsletter that goes "house to house" and its message is very encouraging and spiritually uplifting. I wish I could tell you the stories because they are really good. Some are funny and some are just "slap-you-in-the-face" honest. But that's their stories and these are mine, and this week I decided to go to the church in this area that represents their Christ in the Church philosophy.

Since I was a visitor, I got a little rose to stick on my shirt so everyone would know I needed a little extra attention. They don't believe in having musical instruments so we just sang, or should I say we tried to sing. Anyway the music part wasn't very good, and I think that is their point. It is more about the Gospel and how you are not supposed to change any part of the original Gospel message. Knowing "God's spell" of good tidings is important if you want to receive salvation. God's external powers are clear and proven in nature. These powers should also give us faith of his invisible divine powers and be understood in a way that no man has an excuse for what he does. Your faith will be tested many times. When you need God most, don't turn from your most faithful friend.

There were a lot of old people at this church so I'll use that as a lead in to talk about how they will be taken care of. It takes 14 million Americans working in the health care industry to provide the medical care we already need. This costs Americans about 15% of all of our money (GDP–gross domestic product). This industry will grow by another 20% in the next ten years because now all of the kids born in the "baby boom" generation are getting old. Many of these high-paying jobs don't even require four years of college. With everyone living longer and the cost of fancy medical equipment rising, we will have to make some adjustments soon. There will come a time when the cost for new drugs will be higher than people are willing to pay. The drug benefits won't seem that important to healthy new taxpayers.

Our government's Medicare will have to negotiate with the pharmaceutical companies to buy the drugs that our drug-dependent society has come to "need." They need to purchase them in advance or in large quantities in order to get better deals. There are about 200 types of drugs that can be called "the most popular" for people over 65. Drugs like antidepressants, anti-cholesterol, acid reflux pills, and many others are common and should definitely be purchased in bulk by Medicare since they have to buy them for 42 million people. And when I say "they," I mean us.

There is a lot of profit in the drugs we already have, but if we want to find cures for all the other deadly problems we face, we must let the drug companies make some profit. With more people living longer, the higher the cost will be to the new taxpayers. By 2025, without a war or a major disaster, that number should be around 70 million people needing Medicare drug payments. In order for this medicine to be paid for, we should remember that keeping jobs in America is essential in order to have this tax base to support our Medicare system.

Ch 12

Well this is the Fourth of July weekend and I found a church with "Freedom" in their name! It still amazes me just how many different types of churches there are. And we are so lucky to be born in a free country where we can worship practically any way we want. This was a small group and their sanctuary was in a row of buildings along a busy highway. They were into "praise songs" and many lifted their hands in praise. Everyone was very friendly. A husband and wife are pastors and both are dedicated to spreading "the Word." As we celebrate freedom and America's birthday, all of us should understand how precious freedom is. Those of us who have been locked up, and especially those who are still locked up, have a different appreciation for freedom than people who have never lost theirs.

We often take freedom for granted and it is hard for some of us to imagine life without the internet but over 20 major countries limit internet access. Many of these countries gladly accept our money but they want very little to do with our freedoms. Countries like China, Iran, and Saudi Arabia watch our country and see that too much freedom can demoralize your society and eventually bring down the quality of life. Internet sites that have a non-family or criminal-like theme should at least be put on a separate internet where parents could feel better about their children being on the computer. Freedom that allows pornography and violence to be absorbed on a daily basis simply is not a wise way for society to enjoy the freedom our soldiers have fought and died for. If we are free enough to allow these things, then we should also be free enough to condemn such acts.

Freedom in America is great but we could all learn a thing or two from other countries. There are a few things that need to be corrected in America. Kids with too much freedom can lead to morals that will cause them nothing but trouble, and I don't think that any parent actually wants their children to suffer. But, by being too nice to them you may be setting them up for failure. Violent crime in America is out of control and most of it stems from a lack of good moral values. About 80% of teenage mothers end up living in poverty their whole lives. A new criminal is much younger these days. They often come from single-parent homes and they are angry and very violent. If you don't bring your family back to religion, your children will grow up thinking life is like the songs they listen to or like the wild things they see on their computer. Awful things can be interesting to people who don't know that this is the devil's way of slowly destroying us. Most people should be smart enough to refuse to watch degrading television shows and violent video games.

With the internet, our world is growing closer together. With this happening we really have only two big choices to make so this should be an easy enough question for everyone. Will you come together and work with people who are different from you in order to make the world a better place, or would you rather argue and fight? Even though many people don't like people who are different from them, there really are no other choices. Many times you might "turn up your nose" and dislike someone because of the way they look. But then after a conversation or two and spending some time with that same person, you become friends. So keep this in mind the next time you see someone and notice yourself having a negative attitude for no other reason than the fact they are different looking than most of the people you know. Save your hate as if you only get to use it once and you'll decide to use it more wisely.

In 1776 when the United Colonies began to cut their ties with Britain, the great nation of the United States of America was conceived. Freedom was being made. We wanted freedom from too much government. Five men were put in charge of coming up with a plan. Thomas Jefferson was the Southerner because he was from way down in Virginia. Robert Livingston was from New York. Benjamin Franklin was from Pennsylvania. Roger Sherman was from Connecticut. And John Adams was from Massachusetts. On July 1st, Congress reconvened and they made a few changes to the plan so that finally on July 4th, the Declaration of Independence was made official and about 25 copies were made. Robert Livingston never signed it but eventually 56 delegates did.

We have the freedom to make more laws to limit freedom. We should read the Constitution on a regular basis including the Amendments. In 1787, representatives from most of the states met to produce our governmental principles. The U.S. government only possesses the powers specifically granted to it by the Constitution. Amendments one through ten are known as the Bill of Rights.

Times have changed since 39 men signed those rules. We've grown from four million people to 300 million people. I think only white males were included in making these rules and Benjamin Franklin was the oldest at 81 and the youngest man was Jonathan Dayton at 26. Back then the list of federal crimes was short and if your neighbor did something bad, he just got beat up. Now with another 4,000 federal crime laws, and who knows how many state laws, we are less safe than we were before the "thought police" started running everything.

As I say quite often, "We need to decriminalize 'feel good' crimes where no one is injured and raise the penalties on many other crimes like theft and violence." Decriminalizing laws doesn't make them legal but the fines will help pay for prisons to hold violent people. Prisons for violent people shouldn't be nice and comfortable. A mean violent thief should not be locked up in a nice prison like a man who has worked all of his life and never hurt anyone. And yes, there are many people in prison who have never hurt anyone.

Ch 13

This week I worshipped with Jehovah—or at least with his followers. A few days ago, one of their members came by and invited us to come and worship with them. Since they were on my list of places to visit anyway, I used my personal invitation to add them to my book. Their believers study from the Old Testament or Hebrew scriptures as well as the newer Greek Christian New Testament scriptures, and they consider them historically correct. They believe that Jesus is not God, the world as we know it will soon end, and they don't approve of giving or getting blood.

I sat with a beautiful family and everyone there was incredibly friendly. They study out of a worldwide publication that they print in over 150 languages, and they answer questions from the section they studied during the week. They had a cordless microphone that was handed to each person who was called on to answer each question, and this process included the children. I was surprised at how "the same" they all seemed to be to each other. They were from many different ethnic backgrounds but they dressed similar and acted very similar. They were very calm and pleasant speaking, even the kids! They say we are special to God but as we relate to each other we are much more "all the same!"

I read where Jehovah is called Israel's God. They teach that committing sin need not alienate us from Jehovah God—not if we repent. The dictionary gives the meaning of repent as "to feel regret and to dedicate your life away from sin." Sin is listed as "to offend God by violating His laws."

I remember reading that God gave Moses some laws and even though America has me listed as a criminal, I'm happy to be able to say that I do quite well on God's "Big List" of rules to live by. Gossip is an overlooked sin and is really a big "no-no." It has devastating effects when stories are told about people who aren't around to defend themselves. Each time the stories are told they are twisted more and more to sound more interesting. By being a part of such gossip, you join in on an evil situation which you had no intention of being a part of. By excusing yourself as soon as one of these conversations start, you can stop this bad habit in its tracks.

While I'm writing I'm also watching the World Cup. They show people all over the world in bars drinking and watching the game. Some of these same people in the bars who are having fun will be fighting tomorrow. But today they can find peace and put aside any differences they may have been taught by their parents and friends. On the television I noticed Europe was enjoying a beautiful sunset, and I thought how we would also be enjoying it soon. But it also made me think about how we all have to share the same world. Each of us has the tendency to focus on ourselves and it's easy to forget how everything we do affects someone else. And if we could ever get religion as organized as we have sports, and get as many people as excited about religion as some of them are about sports, well just imagine how many problems that teamwork could fix!

They all seemed so content at this church, but I know that it is not that easy and it takes some effort at first. They say you can find contentment by applying Bible principles. I personally believe that truer words have never been spoken! And that "contentment" is the big prize in life. First Timothy 6 says that we bring nothing into this world and we'll take nothing with us. While we are on this planet, we should be content to have food and clothing; everything else after that is just a bonus. By giving thanks to Jehovah on a regular basis for anything and everything you have, you will remember how blessed you are. Give thanks to good old Jehovah or as he is sometimes called, Yahweh, God, Lord and the creator of the universe.

This universe is the sum of all particles and energy that we think exists. Scientists estimate that there are over one hundred billion galaxies in the universe and each one of those contains millions of stars. And this universe, according to many scientists, is expanding and will someday pop. Everything that our scientists know about the universe is estimated to be only four percent of what seems to exist. Most of the rest is what we call either dark energy or dark matter. Basically dark energy is the opposite of gravity and is a mysterious force that is constantly stretching our universe. Until recently everything our astrophysicists knew about gave off light. Dark matter is everything that seems to be there but doesn't give off light so we can't see it. So that means that 96% of everything still makes the smartest people on Earth go—"huh?" I guess that leaves plenty of space for the existence of heaven.

Ch 14

With all of the trouble making the headlines in the Middle East, crude oil nearing $80 a barrel and gas around $3 a gallon, I think it's time for me to talk about our Muslim friends since they seem to control our transportation future. I don't know about you but I love to cruise in my truck and listen to music, but now it's without the beer. I called them friends but the radical ones are not our friends. Mass violence in the name of religion is a millennia-old theme. Islamic extremism is like a worm in our "apple" of a world. It ruins the fruit of everyone's lives. Islam is one thing in the Middle East that many people have in common. Unfortunately some use this power to abuse people who are desperate.

My journey to a mosque was the farthest one yet, and it was like going on vacation—both because of the distance and how different it was. We took our shoes off so if you go to a mosque, remember to wear good socks. Their religion requires women to cover their hair with what they call a hijab and some require them to cover almost everything else.

They consider dogs "unclean" so don't bring your dog in your truck! Muhammad liked cats but he also said that even a prostitute who gives water to a thirsty dog will get credit toward heaven because her actions show kindness. We were just visitors so we watched them kneel and pray. Afterwards they let us sample different types of Middle Eastern food. It was a very interesting night and it felt very good and holy. It furthered my interest and desire in my quest to examine more religions.

There are so many similarities in each religion. Many of which have the same principles with different names. Since this trip, I have studied some history which teaches us many important lessons that we should apply to our lives today. One very interesting part of history is the Ottoman Empire as they conquered the Christians in their area. Surprisingly when I called my father this morning, he said he had visited a mosque. I told him about the Ottoman Empire and about their attack on the Christians. He said the Muslims where he went were against killing anything that was alive so there must be several types of Islam just like there are several types of Christianity. I just don't understand why Muslims kill Muslims. That should definitely be against their religion.

The Muslim religion is the second largest in the world at 22%. Over 95% of those Muslims are peaceful. The different sects of Islam are mixed with politics and this is the reason for most of the violence. Allah is their word for God. A man named Muhammad was thought to be a prophet. And it looks like Sunnis believe that Ali was Allah's friend and Muhammad's son-in-law. Sunnis believe Ali was the fourth and last of the "guided caliphs." A caliph had full political and religious power. But after Muhammad, you had Abu Bakr, then Umar, and then Uthman who were leading the Muslims. Shia or Shi'ite comes from Shiat Ali. They believe that Ali should have been the first caliph and then only Muhammad's direct descendents should rule. It is said that Uthman was murdered at prayer. Then Ali took over as caliph. Uthman's cousin, Mu'awiya Ummayad, was the governor of Damascus and during a confrontation with Ali, the Mu'awiyas stuck verses of the Quran on their spears. Ali's supporters refused to fight them so he had to make a deal with Mu'awiya. One of Ali's people saw this as betrayal and killed him. Mu'awiya took over as caliph after Ali's oldest son was paid off and later poisoned. Their sons both fought for rule and the Shia and Sunni division was set. I still see nothing in all of this that is worth killing anyone over, but the two sides have been fighting ever since.

I've noticed in prison that most new converts to Islam are black and a quarter of the six million Muslims in America are black. With homicide being the number one cause of death in black men today, I can't help but wonder where all of this hate comes from. All types of young people are committing violent crimes and they seem to have no remorse or regret for hurting so many people including the victims' families. I'm sure without the drugs there would be less violence. I know if you are doing dope, you get very tired, mean and crazy. If you're selling dope, a lot of people are always looking for you and you get on a power trip. This "mighty" feeling will end with a rude awakening if you live long enough to make it to prison.

Many parents are in prison and their kids are growing up without their love. They grow up with violent music and they think life is meaningless. Murder, sex, abortion, and robbery are as common in their short lives as going out to dinner is to most people. We cannot continue to say that it is not our problem. We cannot continue to blame others.

One reason our crime rate is not worse than it is, is because a thousand more people a week are sent to prison than are released. And even if you are only sent to prison for a nonviolent drug or alcohol crime, chances are when you get out, you will be bitter and violent. After wasting a lot of time, you will leave prison with little or no training to improve your chances at having what most people take for granted as a normal life. I think if you don't learn some kind of way to make a living, you should have to stay in prison until you do—because when you get out, if you don't get a job, your chances of committing a crime are almost certain. For most former inmates, going to church or mosque or whichever type you choose, is the best way to stay out of prison. Since most Muslims are non-violent, I think the 13 million moderate Muslims in Europe could do much more toward helping these violent communities.

I noticed in prison how easy it is to start a religious future and they all teach love not hate. Of the six million Americans that practice Islam, some are immigrants and some are American born—some are Democrats and some are

Republicans. The local leaders of the world's top three major religions got together to sign a "Declaration of Peace." In Iraq hundreds of tribal chiefs signed a pact to work towards peace. Almost all Saudis are Muslims and they should be able to help us if they wanted to. In Saudi Arabia, the Mattawan enforce strict puritanical Wahhabi Islamic code on their streets and keep the peace. The Saudis do help us in one way—they return a little of our oil money in the way of students. The Saudis love to send their children to college in America, so they should be willing to help us with the Islamic instability even though most Arabs in America aren't Muslim. Each scholarship Saudis give costs them about thirty thousand dollars. If they send us 15,000 students, that's $45 million for U.S. colleges. Now if we could combine some understanding with all of this education, maybe we could find a way to stop some of the killing and suffering because of a twisted form of Islamic religion. With all of their oil money, Iran (the Shiites) and Saudi Arabia (the Sunnis) are playing "war games" in Iraq and we are just in the way.

Most of the one billion Muslims are in Indonesia and India. I think there are the Shiite, Sunni, Baha'ia, Sufi, Druze, Isma'ilite, Alawite, Musayri, and much fewer Kurds since the rule of Saddam Hussein. Iran is actually ruled by Shiite clerics. Shiites let clerics interpret the Quran however they want. It seems to me that the radical Shiites in Iran stir up the most trouble. But most of the world's one billion Muslims aren't Shiite. In Iraq, the Sunnis oppose a proposal that would give authority to Shiites in the oil-rich south. In Iraq, the Sunni Arab insurgency has raged out of control since Saddam Hussein's capture. Sunni snipers shot at Shiite parades in Baghdad while they were on their way to the golden-domed shrine of Imam Moussa Kadhim who is one of the twelve Shiite Muslim saints. During Saddam Hussein's Sunni rule, Shiites were forbidden to assemble in public.

Now the Shiite militias and some members of the legislature wage their own private local wars. Iraq's Prime Minister, Nouri al-Maliki, is Shiite and he went to Iran to work on a 24-point reconciliation plan that he hopes will bridge the gap between religious, ethnic and political groups. The vice-president is a Sunni Arab and he also is trying to get the insurgency to stop the violence. The Iraqi Islamic Party is the main Sunni political force and they blame the Shiite militias for the bloodshed. Another Sunni party is called the Accordance Front. One of the Shiite militias is the Mahdi Army led by Muqtada al-Sadr and then another one—that is said to be just a "political force,"—is the Badr Brigade. Some other political groups are the Taliban, Hezbollah, Baath, Fatah, Hamas, and Likud. Peace would end their importance. The Shia Iranian Ayatollah Kohmeini preached that jihad is needed to make people obedient. They speak of the sword but now that has been replaced with much deadlier weapons. The Sunni al-Qaida's Osama Bin Laden wants all infidels to convert to Islam or die. They consider an infidel as a person with a different religious faith or no faith at all.

Meanwhile in Lebanon, a Sunni Prime Minister and a Shiite Hezbollah militant spoke together against Israel. So it seems that when it benefits the two sects they can get along. Hezbollah is sponsored by Syria and Iran and those two are supplied by China and Russia. China should be helping us in Iraq. With China's growth in manufacturing, they get a lot of American money. Since we buy so many products made in China, they are now buying more cars and they need all the oil they can get. So—since we wouldn't pay a little more for American-made products, our money will now go for higher gas. Americans are more concerned about how much beer their otherwise good neighbor drinks or what a movie star or sports star is doing than the fact that every time they go shopping they buy hundreds of dollars of goods that are made in China. This was our money and someday it could be used to destroy our way of life.

Radical Muslims take advantage of our conceit and greed, and Muslims blame everyone but the Muslims for the world's problems. Muslim extremists take advantage of other Muslims by warning them of other religions' evil agendas. Their ideology of "brainwash-by-the-way-of-the-Koran" says they support no peace with any non-Muslim, but I have yet to see a verse that says to kill anyone. Islam means surrender. To surrender to Islam is to change your whole social pattern for the good of the community. The Koran, or Quran in Arabic, is supposed to be the message of God revealed to Mohammad. Mohammad accused the Jews of misinterpreting the Bible and rejecting Jesus who had been sent by Allah to show the Jews the mistakes they had made. Mohammad accused the Christians of blasphemy by humiliating Eissa on the cross. Eissa, whom we call Jesus, was one of their prophets. Shiites believe a Sunni poisoned the saint Mohammad in 799 A.D. They are so willing to die for Islam as they shout "God bless Muhammad" but it just doesn't make much sense to me.

For America to fight a war where the enemy doesn't wear a uniform is the ultimate in stupidity. They might as well be invisible and how can you defeat what you cannot see. Like the drug war at home, it can defeat us from both sides. We unsuccessfully try to lock up everyone who wants to escape reality. And by not teaching our children right from wrong—partly because of the fear of being locked up for "spanking"—the children are easy targets of mostly foreign supplied drug dealers. Not that I support spanking, but by removing it, many kids won't learn any discipline until they get to prison. With our combined purchases of drugs, clothes, electronics and oil, we are supporting our own defeat. The Muslim jihadists are taught this and are told that one day the world will be theirs. Even our philanthropists, who got rich from American dollars, are now sending that money overseas.

Someday we'll have to pull our ostrich heads out of the oily Middle East sand and decide what is more important.

We'll have to make some tough decisions. Walk to work or find energy at home. Work to help drug addicts or take care of them and their families for the rest of their lives. We should make our products locally even if they cost a little more, and we could do without having so many different styles and so many foreign-made toys. It will be sadly ironic if years from now, historians discover that the "foreign-made" toys we purchased to make our children happy helped pay for a war that destroyed them. If Americans are buying mostly foreign-made products, we shouldn't be surprised when our economy falters. The "money vacuum" is sucking the life out of America and our enemies are waiting for us to implode. We send our money for oil and then some of it makes its way for weapons that kill our young men and women. I guess it will have to get much worse before the rich are affected enough to want to change how the money is spent. At this rate, much worse may be just what we get.

Ch 15

This week I went back to the town where my old house is and to the "Rock" church. They have some really big churches in other cities and this one is growing too. I went here with my wild young girlfriend before I got locked up. I was trying to get her to settle down and one of my rules was that we go to church. Needless to say, the drugs beat us both so now I'm back for another dose of religion!

This church is very upbeat and I think almost anyone would enjoy it. I'm still amazed at how all these churches get filled. There were a lot of young people at this church which I think is very important for any church. We all know that our children are the future and to let them grow up in a sin-filled world is really selfish on our part. We don't have to live in the future but they do.

When I was young I thought I was indestructible since I could "party" all day and all night and my body would heal. I now realize how vulnerable I am and how that healing process is part of the miracle that should reinforce our faith in a higher power. What if you were born to do something great or be a great leader, but along the way your addiction changed history. Did your addiction only affect you? Probably not! And there is no way to know for sure but the odds are that you would have helped society more if you had stayed off dope. Now that I'm off dope, I'll try to help everyone through my writing of this book and all of the other things I continue to do. You may not agree with everything in this book, and then again you might. Whether you do or don't, I hope that it makes you do something. Remember that seeing it in a book or in the newspaper or on television doesn't make it true or right. It is still just someone's story and it's up to you to determine what is best for you.

Laws that you may not agree with are in place because others felt stronger about them than you do. People who complain about things are only complaining to themselves if they don't get out and get involved. In the Bible, Paul said, "a time will come when our teachers and leaders will tell us what we want to hear so they can meet their own desires." Christians must stick with the way Jesus teaches. And it wouldn't hurt everyone else either. Jesus doesn't put down any religions or anyone. From this day forth try harder to live as you believe Jesus or your personal higher power would want you to.

I always thought that life would get easier the older I got but at 48, I'm finding out that isn't the case. I see now how important it is for young people to focus seriously on their lives while they have the chance to influence their futures. Time wasted partying will only make your future harder because the older you get, the harder it is to do a lot of things. Then when you're grown, and as your parents and kids get older, they'll have problems that will need your time and attention. Saving and planning for the future will make your life more enjoyable. After taking care of your health and spiritual well-being, saving money is the most important thing you can do to make your life better. Once you have some money saved up, you can slowly start to buy the things you would like without having to charge and pay interest or take out a loan. But the fewer things you buy, the less complicated your life will be. Simplicity and staying out of trouble will be one of the most beneficial lessons you can learn if you want to enjoy your life.

Ch 16

This week I went to a church whose name sounds like Jesus' home of Nazareth. I know there's a Nazareth, Pennsylvania, and I used to listen to Nazareth on my eight-track stereo in my '67 Camaro. However, this was my first church with a name like that. It was pretty much like most churches except this week I got lucky and there was a man and his wife visiting and singing and giving their testimony.

Riding with Jesus is the trip of a lifetime! The couple had to drive a long way just to get here and you have to admire them for that alone. He played the trombone (just like my granddad did) and in the past he had played with a lot of famous people. He had some good stories about choices he had to make in his life between Jesus and fame/fortune, and stories about personal tragedies which always test your faith. They told some really sad family stories that made you wonder how they could cope with it all.

We are new people after we have decided to live as Jesus, as well as other people in the Bible, would like us to. Some call it *Born Again*. We will still think about many things that we had to give up and we may still slip in areas that we shouldn't. But we will always have Jesus to call on when we need extra strength and we can straighten up our lives again knowing that he died for our sins so that we may enjoy a future life someday. Jesus will always forgive you if you ask. Then you need to do your part so your life will find a path that leads you to a good point.

I just opened a cold soda pop! In prison we were lucky if we got a hot one. It reminded me to thank the Lord and ask him to please help me do the right things so I can stay out of that crazy place they call prison. If your family raised you right, you'll have good roots and after prison, you'll be able to grow back straight and strong. All Satan needs is a split second and without you even realizing it, he will begin to take away your happiness and change it to boredom, hatred, envy and ungratefulness. And if you run with thieves, plan on getting robbed. In other words, choose your "friends" very carefully. Sometimes it's better to be lonely than to hang around people who will damage your goals in life. When I first entered prison I actually didn't have anything except warm water. I didn't even have a cup. Then I moved up in the world when a guy gave me an old plastic water bottle and some coffee. I didn't have any hot water so I had to be happy with warm and cold coffee.

In prison you have plenty of time to think, but genius borders on insanity when you try to figure everything out. I never did anything bad enough to deserve this kind of treatment. Millions of people have lived and died. Even animals have been happy and sad. Yet the world doesn't make any more sense today after all the lessons of time. If our lives are just a split second of eternity, then why should we care how we live? But if our lives are how we will be judged for eternity, then shouldn't we at least be grateful for whatever is happening? And once you are grateful you will be happier. Once you are happy you can beat Satan. Is it that easy? Maybe not, but close your eyes for a while and imagine that you own nothing and there is nothing there. Just sit and relax for a minute. Now open your eyes and think about everything you see. If you try, you'll be amazed at the complexity of everything. You'll be amazed at what has been created since time began. Be thankful and enjoy it all!

Remember, believing in anything takes an open mind but not a gullible mind. By studying factual history, you can see how societies have suffered from bad choices. Studying past societies will let you and others make personal conclusions on many subjects. Keep in mind that many times in a person's life their views on a subject may change. And while you believe what you believe, always leave your mind open. Someday you may be shocked to find out that you were wrong the whole time, but it's better to find out late than not at all.

Ch 17

This week my mom went to church with me! We went to a type of church she used to go to when we both lived in the "Big City!" Today we had to drive about 30 miles to the closest city to find this kind of church. I had heard of this church (whose name starts with a U), and I was expecting a rather normal church-going morning.

As it turned out, this group might be more of a religious movement than a type of church. This local ministry group met in a real nice remodeled house, but it is much smaller than I had expected—compared to their big church in the big city.

We got lucky again because they had a guest speaker. She had us close our eyes and she led us on a meditation-type lesson. The first thing that came to my mind was that all we needed was to "fire up a joint" and it would be just like the hippies and beatniks in the sixties. She said we should all be patient—like the farmer who must wait for his precious fruit. She talked about "chakras" which are energy centers and astrology and how this century is different from the last one. They mentioned that we are children of God, but I never heard them mention anything about Jesus.

They gave us a Visitor/Welcome Packet which looks real nice so let me see what's in it! I thought I felt a cassette tape! I'll listen to it later. A card says there are many names for God, and many paths and ways to worship Him. They say that they are not a denomination, but more of a group of students who study a metaphysical philosophy based on the Bible. With all the problems in the world, they teach that we must work together for answers and solutions that contribute to the betterment of the world.

I finally found a reference to Jesus in their paperwork which says they teach a practical understanding of his teachings. Much emphasis is placed on how your thoughts, feelings, and actions determine how your day and your life will unfold.

When I was locked up, I had planned on starting my day with meditation and picturing what I wanted to accomplish each day. But since I have been out, I have been so busy that each day is scheduled with more than I can accomplish. Someday when I get my life back to a point where I was before I was locked up, I can slow down and meditate each morning and focus on a few good things that I would like to accomplish. Until then this book is on the top of my big "to do" list—while also making some money. After that, yard work and household chores fill my days. When I was locked up, I dreamed of someday being able to do all of this—even the chores!

Now that I am off dope, I can really dream! Not only can I make plans for my future but I can actually follow through with those plans. But what I really want to talk about is what happens when my body shuts down at night. Now my dreams are so realistic and complex. I think about them each time I wake up—with all the twists and turns the plot takes. They are so wild that it would be very hard to write a story like them. I dream of old friends that I haven't seen in years. One time I remember a friend showing me their old pictures and it was all incredibly accurate. One time I was even asleep, dreaming another dream in my dream! If this can happen when your body is asleep, it is not that far fetched to see the possibilities of "heaven." Since the universe is full of electrical currents just like your brain, and if all of these stories can take place while you're dead asleep, imagine what might happen when your body finally shuts down for good!

My favorite part of this group's literature is where they emphasize having "no judgment!" I hear that from all of the pastors and preachers but have yet to see a church where all of the members can honestly say that they follow this very important Jesus-directed philosophy. With all I've learned, sometimes it's still hard for me, but I'm trying.

I do know that what you feel in your heart is what's important for you to have a happy life. If you have yet to find a place to focus on your divine potential, this church would be an excellent place to call Your Home Church!

Ch 18

I saw something on television about a Mormon so I thought it would be interesting this week if I could find a Mormon church. Well I was sort of surprised to find a Jesus Christ of Latter Day Saints Church in the same little town as my house/shop. Their sign is kind of small and I had to ask some people in another car if this was the right church. The first one to speak was a little boy and he answered very proudly, "This is the church of Jesus Christ Latter Day Saints!"

The Mormons have Priests, Bishops and Elders. These Elders are young men from other states who are living here for two years and doing residency for their faith. One of them showed me around and gave me his card. I was wondering about the multiple wife deal and I learned that "Fundamentalist" Mormons consider polygamy a religious tenet or belief. Those Mormons had legal wives and spiritual wives. Most LDS churches disavowed this practice in 1890. They consider themselves a separate Christian religion and follow "First Century Christianity" which was set up by the Roman emperor Constantine after Tiberius had the religious teacher Jesus of Galilee executed. The foundation of most Christian religions is based on the fact that Jesus was resurrected three days later to sit with God and will someday return.

Once again, everybody at this church was especially nice, and they are very focused on the family which, being an only child, I do not have much of. Most of them practice home schooling which I am a big fan of. Learning *bad* things is usually more interesting than learning *good* things and one kid in a class can corrupt a whole group of kids. Teaching kids at home can keep bad actions from multiplying and home schooling will teach kids important values that only hard work and a family can teach.

Jesus didn't have a formal education either. He was just a man from Nazareth in a desolate section of the Roman Empire. There weren't any famous people or even anyone impressive from there at all. Jesus boldly claimed "to be the light of the world" which would have been a crazy claim for anyone. Without the help of newspapers, television, or the internet, how could he have thought this? I guess good news traveled fast!

I know that Joseph Smith founded this church and he wanted to be the President or King of America. He founded Nauvoo, Illinois. He wrote a book in 1830 that is their other "bible" called the Book of Mormon. But unlike the Bible, many of the events in it might have taken place in the Americas. Like all good books, it has been changed over time. It is available in over 70 languages. Mormon was another "prophet" who lived in the 4th Century and he was "visited" by Jesus Christ. Then Mormon's son, Morini "visited" Joseph Smith over a century later. Supposedly during these "visits" your body heats up and you feel "all that is right." What I read of the Book of Mormon was quite interesting and someday I'll read the rest of it. Like in every religion, Joseph really believed in these principles. It would be very hard to make up all of this, and like every good book, I recommend that you read it. It's a little different from the stories of Jesus and other stories in the King James—and other versions—of the Bible. The days of Jesus Christ were very wild times. Well now that I think about it, what times aren't wild?

Joseph Smith's Thirteen Articles of Faith is his creed of fundamental doctrines they live by. It's similar to other doctrines. Number one says, "We believe in God the Eternal Father, His son Jesus Christ, and in the Holy Ghost." The main LDS Temple is in Salt Lake City and to enter you must possess a "Temple Recommended" entry pass. So that leaves most of us out of that visit. Most members have only one wife but Joseph thought you should have more and there are also many instances of this practice in the Old Testament. As long as they are all over 18 and happy, I don't see any problem with this except that in America it is illegal so that answers that for now. Does anyone believe in having more than one husband? What would be the benefits of having more than one "significant other" and what would be the drawbacks? Is it about sex or would they provide other needs? Throughout time, young women have always been more attractive to men, and I don't think it should be so surprising to anyone. God or Yahweh designed it that way to populate the Earth.

There are many different ways of doing things and just because someone does something different from the way you do it doesn't mean that it's the wrong way. It may aggravate you but that is only the "devil" trying to make you mad. We should thank God that we are all different because it would be very boring if we weren't. The people you love and like to be with will do things different from the way you do them. Accept this as a blessing and overcome your problem with it as a welcomed challenge if you wish to stay with this person or these people. And remember—no one is perfect. And if you are waiting for that perfect mate before you get married, you will live your life alone.

❧Ch 19❧

This week I went to one of God's assemblies! The church sign said, "Putting the Christ Back in Christian." I think all of the Christian churches wish they could do that with their members. It is one thing to be what you think is a good person but to live a Jesus-fashioned life is much harder. We can never be *good enough* or as good as Jesus—or however you want to say it. But we could try harder to be more like Jesus would want us to be. I think some of the most abused or overlooked teachings are the ones about judging and forgiveness. Everyone seems to fall short on both of these even if they do everything else perfectly. I do better on forgiveness than I do on judging. I try not to judge sloppy-looking people but when I see people acting like "wanna-be gangsters," I wish I could take them to prison to meet all of the past "gangsta's" and let them see the future this sorry excuse for a life-style will get them. Even some pro athletes will try to act "fly" and imitate the gangsta moves they see in the videos. If they only knew how that little bit of disrespect for a Holy life-style plays into the hands of the devil.

I got lucky today because the children had a special, and they stayed with us all morning instead of going to children's church. I always wished I had a kid. First I wanted a little boy like me, but now I'd rather have a daughter. They are just so cute and more fun to take shopping. But as life is, I didn't get what I wanted because abortion has always prevented it. Now there is a chance that one might be mine but since I just got out of prison, I haven't gotten around to taking the test to prove it one way or the other. The lady who has her hasn't even let me see her. But I have learned to put everything in God's hands and to take care of what I am supposed to take care of. Everything else will fall into place at a better time. I do know she's in good hands and being taken care of. If I start drinking too much beer or smoking dope, then I wouldn't be very good as a father anyway. So it's best that I follow my plan and stay out of trouble.

I write several people in prison and it's a very good way to keep motivated. It reminds me of how good I have it and it actually makes you *high* on life. At the church today, I watched a video on inner-city projects. They buy old houses right in the middle of the drug dealers' "hoods" and turn them into churches for the children. The kids talk about how they grow up with their parents gone all the time. They know their parents are on drugs and at night they cry themselves to sleep all alone. Most people watch this stuff and find it hard to believe. Those of us who have been on drugs don't find it hard to believe. Most of the pastors of these inner-city church projects have been on drugs and they've managed to get their lives straightened out. So it is possible to get off drugs, but very few do. Most will live in prison or they'll die from their addiction.

Some estimates are that addiction costs Americans about $500 billion a year which is more than any other sickness. And this doesn't count the loss of productivity from workers or should I say non-workers! Drug use is the cause of over half the crime in America. I read how in Afghanistan they are making more opium for heroin than ever before. We have given that country millions of dollars to end this problem, but they must be using the money to plant more poppies. Heroin, Meth, and Crack are the biggest contributors to our declining society. We lose 13 billion American dollars a year to Mexico and Canada for marijuana. Over 20 countries get most of their income from "drugs." Spending more time teaching the wealthy kids about drug abuse would be a good defense. They have more money and they are the ones who pay for the fancy cars that the drug dealers drive. Sadly tons of poor kids are learning this message from their own parents who spend all of their money on dope. If the middle class and rich kids don't see this disaster up close and personal at home, they will easily have enough money to start their own addiction and drug-dealing business. By locking up everyone who gets high, the only time the kids get to see drug dealers is when they are on the "top of their game." It all looks so glamorous on the videos and sounds so cool in the songs. Surely we sober people are smart enough to develop some type of program that keeps parents out of long-term prison sentences and into a program that can be used to let people see what really happens when you choose to live a wild life-style. I've said before that simple druggies who can't do their probation, and have no other crimes, need to be put together so they can tell each other their horror stories while their in prison. After a year and a half, put them into a six-month program where young people can meet them and learn the real facts about dope. If the prisoners do well on this program, let them go home. If they get out and screw up, then they go back for twice as long as before. It will make the court system much simpler. I've said things like this before but I truly believe in this type of program since I've been in prison and have seen how even the biggest drug dealers are broken after a couple of years. If two years doesn't fix them, then maybe four will. If four doesn't work, I'll bet the next eight or sixteen will!

Once again, this "God" church was and is an excellent choice for anyone looking for a good place to be with good people. They believe in Jesus' virgin birth, sinless life, all of the miracles, his death for our sins, his rise after death, and his return someday for a thousand year rule. This group believes in God the Father, God the Son, and God the Holy Spirit which to me seems to cover it all. They say the law of the Lord is perfect and I tend to agree. It is definitely better than any alternative—the alternative being a life of hell. And if you don't believe me, just look around. The constant search for something to make you happy is enough to drive anyone crazy. By accepting the bad things that happen to you in life, you are at peace and not out causing more problems on top of the things you can't control. Counting on a future with Jesus helps too and keeps you from being scared of death.

Ch 20

This week we went to one of the churches with Science in their name. It is one of the more traditional ones and it was founded by a woman. They refer to the Mother Church often with emphasis on living a moral life. The dictionary states that "moral," as an adjective, is being concerned between the differences involved in right and wrong ways of life. But it still doesn't tell us much about what moral really means other than something about sexual responsibility being the most important. I guess we can all determine our own stages of right and wrong, good and bad, and most people know the difference. But just knowing the difference is not usually enough for us to choose what we know would be the best thing to do. We often "close our eyes" when things don't conveniently fit into our normal fun lives. Many times we know that we should do something but that would cost us time or money and we conveniently move on down the road. We quickly think of something else in order to rationalize why we can't do something that Jesus would probably do in that same circumstance. Another word that comes to mind is virtue. The definition of "virtue" states it is qualities possessing great moral values and also something about female chastity. Well it's lucky for me that I am one of those who believe in monogamy. I guess if I'm lucky enough to find another mate, I will still value her enough to be totally devoted like I always have. Unfortunately the women I've been with haven't been as kind to me, and that—plus drugs and prison—is why I'm still single. I almost never lie and I don't steal which must be on the "top ten" morally correct list. Hey, I bet the Ten Commandments is a good list of morals!

Well back to this week's church. The founder was big on "the mind healing the body." I think we can all vouch for the fact that it's possible to tell yourself to be happy or you can just sit around being bored. At this church they read from the bible and then they read from their book with corresponding thoughts and ideas. Their book of health and science has sold ten million copies in over 15 languages. She writes about how women can be leaders of men without having to sacrifice their bodies. People will only be valuable in life if they value themselves. When you lower your standards, the next step you take is surely to be even lower. They say we should fear the Lord but I imagine that they are referring to His power that demands respect. Don't be silent; sing praise to the Lord so that all will know your thanks unto Him. Believe that Jesus died for our sins to save us. Believe that he died and rose again, and so will you. We must believe that somehow, some way, we shall live again.

Being a scientist church, I got to thinking about science. Science is knowledge gained by observation and the deductions that are acquired from these methods and principles. These deductions are made in a part of your central nervous system called the brain. It is a marvel that is beyond an easy scientific explanation. Without a brain our lives would be as senseless as a plant. Many people take their brain for granted. They think that being born and having intelligence was owed to them. They waste their thoughts on sad things that ruin their health. Scientists have learned how they think the brain works. Many scientists think that all of creation was an accident. It would be very hard for our brains and everything else to have turned out the way it did by accident. However it is possible for many things to have further evolved the way some scientists claim. For everything, including the brain, to have formed and worked so well would be nothing short of a miracle. The brain tells us everything we do including many things that we don't even notice. The three main areas of the brain are the cerebrum, cerebellum, and the brain stem. The largest area is the cerebrum which controls most of our actions. The cerebellum keeps everything in the body working like it should. The brain stem has many parts and features and is probably the most complicated of all. The brain only weighs about three pounds but it uses one-fifth of your body's energy. It has over 100 billion nerve cells and each one of those has countless connections to other cells. It controls the muscles by releasing acetylcholine which then swims a small gap and tells the muscles what to do. The brain is a very complex "super computer." There is much more to it, and this book is designed to get your brain thinking and to help people who are on dope or who knows somebody on dope. I've learned that the more I use my brain the less interest I have in doing anything that would alter my mood. By searching for things that are interesting to you, you just might find what really makes you happy. I know drugs won't do it.

◆Ch 21◆

It is starting to cool off from the summer heat, so I put on my brand new long-sleeve shirt and went to the local Catholic Church. This chapter in the book could be the largest one since there are so many Catholics and they do so many things including having some very good schools. But I think I'll choose to leave some of it out and try to keep this chapter short. Today's little church was packed, but out here in the country most of the people were dressed casually. This church is much smaller than the big Catholic Church I went to in the big city when I was young. That big Catholic Church was very impressive and very formal and both of them seemed a little more complicated than the churches I went to when I was growing up. A lady sitting next to me helped me with the readings and rituals. Some churches let all of their children go to Children's Church, but here the children stayed in church with the adults. It was a little rambunctious but everyone seemed used to it and it didn't bother me at all. We folded down a padded rail to kneel and pray. When we took communion we all went down to the front for the bread, and they had real wine which was a shock since I had quit drinking. I don't know if I was supposed to share this with the Catholics, but I didn't have a chance to find out so I did. On the way out, there was Holy Water to splash on your head which was another surprise.

The Pope I had always heard of was Pope John Paul II. The new German pope, Pope Benedict XVI "caught hell" when he just repeated what many Muslims have said about "living by the sword!" If beheading isn't evil then I don't know what you would call evil. Those "poor misunderstood" radical Muslims can use anything and spin it to their advantage! So the Pope invited Muslim leaders from several nations to join him at his summer residence to work on any misunderstandings they may have. He urges diplomats to refuse to send money to any group that supports violence in the name of faith. These leaders may want to work together but the poorer radical extremist followers are the ones that need a leader to guide them in a positive direction. Benedict also plans on a trip to work on relations between the Vatican and other Orthodox churches, and he is leading a campaign for religious liberty which includes all Christians, even in countries like China and Saudi Arabia.

Developing countries learn many things from American culture including the bad stuff like our lowering of family values and abortion. Catholics have a strict prohibition on abortion. This type of abortion is the termination of life to an unborn child. In the book of Jeremiah in the Bible, it says that before the Lord formed you in the womb, he knew you. When I think of a baby being aborted I see it waving "no thanks" and "moon dancing" in reverse like Michael but singing the old Bee Gees song—"Stayin' Alive." Some people think that sex is just a sport. Fewer and fewer people seem to be in favor of indiscriminate abortions that are required for no reason other than the fact that they had sex and got pregnant. The last Supreme Court vote was almost split down the middle which would have been in favor of eliminating the shameful destruction of the 46 million fetuses since Roe vs. Wade in 1973. And now if you kill a pregnant mother, you are charged with two murders so what does that tell you?

Now I don't want to support anything that would be twisted into a baby factory but I do know that there are a lot of people who would like to have a child. Maybe if a woman had an option of abortion or benefiting from the birth, they might continue a pregnancy and let the baby be born. I'm just trying to come up with anything that would let more babies survive. I know I'm glad I wasn't aborted! Having so many abortions just doesn't make sense when scientists and their companies are charging $2,000 a year to store frozen embryos for a family. About half a million embryos are stored in the United States. Then you have sperm banks, egg donors and fertility treatments. It is a multi-billion dollar business created by the need for babies.

Also a major birth control policy worldwide is needed to lessen the suffering of children who are living with a family that never had the means to raise them properly. By reducing the number of people born in "unlivable" conditions, governments would then have a chance to work together to provide jobs to eliminate extreme poverty for millions of people in all areas of the world.

Ch 22

This week I went to the Baptist church closest to where I live. It's also one of the first places I went to when I got out of prison because I had to go to a Celebrate Recovery meeting for parole and that was on a Monday evening.

However this Sunday evening, they had a special worship because several of the churches in the area joined together for a nondenominational get-together. A pastor from another church where I now attend Celebrate Recovery was the speaker. He talked about how others look at Christians to see if what they have is worth leading the dedicated faithful life that most so-called Christians try to live. And he talked about how many of us fall short in portraying a positive attitude when things go wrong. No matter what happens, a true Christian should not get upset because we have the glory of Jesus Christ to be happy about. Follow Jesus and keep him in sight because when you lose sight, you cannot expect to go the right way. Jesus saves but until then you also have to save yourself. And don't forget to thank the preacher; it will help him next time!

Psalms is one of my least favorite books in the Bible. However one of my favorite verses in Psalms is 118:24 which says, "This is the day the Lord has made so let's rejoice and be glad in it." In other words, don't take your day for granted. Awake and realize all there is to enjoy. Look on the bright side even if you have to put on your sunglasses.

You can work hard to be Christ-like but all the work in the world won't get you to heaven. You must accept Jesus in your heart, learn to forgive everyone, and feel sadness for the discontent in people you meet. Until you learn to do this, your *dark side* will sabotage your best intentions. When you finally feel the grace of Jesus' type of love for everybody, then you will know why your life has been so difficult in the past. When this day comes to your life, you'll be able to focus on that feeling and be at peace with yourself and the world.

Accepting Jesus' love is similar to meditation in a way because it puts you in a relaxed state of mind. Deep breathing helps too by getting more oxygen into your system which is very important since most of us barely use our lungs. Once again I'm no expert but here's what I've learned. The amount of oxygen in your cells helps prevent cancer. Every cell in your body is surrounded by lymph. Breathing controls the lymph fluid which is full of white blood cells that protect your body. You have about four times as much lymph fluid as you do blood. When the blood is pumped through the heart, it carries oxygen and nutrients to the capillaries. The dead cells and other toxic material are neutralized and removed by the lymph. So once again, God has designed a system that would be hard for any of us to have dreamed up. God has filled the world with so many different things and lessons for us to learn from each one. God will give you a rock to stand on but he'll also make you look for it! Enjoy your day and realize how many amazing things are happening all around you.

Ch 23

The weather is cool and it is like heaven on Earth! I would say that it's a great day to be free, but every day is a great day to be free. Maybe today is just a great day to be outside. But when I was locked up I couldn't wait until the day came when I was able to go out and stand in the rain. There hasn't been much rain around here this summer, but it is supposed to rain today! It's Sunday, but I've already gone to church this week for this book. Several days ago, I went to a special study group on Hinduism.

So I am staying home today because I really need to work on this book (and watch the NASCAR Final Ten). Today is Constitution Day, September 17, the day in 1787 that some of the most educated Americans got together to outline how our country should work. I don't see anything in the Constitution that lets our government take our money and give it away on objects of benevolence like Medicaid, business subsidies, or any type of welfare. Churches used to take care of the less fortunate but now I guess we want the government to run every part of our lives.

The middle of the middle-class income for a person in America is $43,000 a year or about $825 a week. The federal budget this year, which is our money, is about $2.5 trillion and about two-thirds of that is spent helping those who seem to need help. About a third of that tax money comes from hard-working people and goes to people who could work and provide for themselves. I'm glad to see some improvement is finally being made in that area. The Constitution doesn't have any authority to provide for charity and has only become the duty of the government because of what is referred to as "good for the general welfare of the public." A century ago our government ran on 2% of our nation's income (GDP). Now it takes 20% and if we don't put a stop to it, there won't be any money left to run any businesses other than the government.

America's poor are not like other countries' poor. Our poor overeat, watch television and just like the wealthy, they complain. Other countries can make products cheaper than the United States because their people don't have time to complain since they have to work very hard just so they will be able to eat. Approximately 44 million Americans are on Medicaid and some of those could work if they had to. New York alone spends about $40 billion of our $2.5 trillion on their Medicaid assistance.

Now back to the church I visited this week where we studied Hinduism. Hinduism is a very old religion, and they have many different varieties with their own sacred texts. Once again, I am no expert but here is a fast version of what I got out of the group. Hinduism evolved from many beliefs and traditions around 4,000 B.C., but the oldest document to survive is called the Rig-Veda or Vedas from the Vedic religion. The Aryans traveled a lot. Some ended up around what is now known as Ireland, others around Iran whose name comes from Aryan. Their worship of gods led us to the mythological stories many of us learned as kids. Others settled in India and the stories of Hindu gods have many similarities. They believe in a super-cosmic spirit, or god, who is beyond our time and space. They call this spirit Brahman, but they call him (or her) Ishvara.

We'll use the male gender in this article and if you want to say her in place of him, I don't mind. He or she is the reason for everything and he has no beginning and no end. We only exist because of His thoughts or consciousness, and we are trying to return to Him. Everything is His and therefore should be treated as such, with compassion for all life.

They also have Divas which are like semi-gods or angels. Many different types of labor groups have their own Divas that they sort of worship or ask for help. To me that sounds like it would be mentally strengthening and could help you get your job done. Our duty, or dharma, is to learn why we should do "good works." The effort we make is called "yoga" and also involves physical and mental exercises that move our focus from ourselves to others and God. These good deeds build up our karma and after we die, our karma will determine our next life. They believe our spirits will exist for eternity, and they are not totally separate from God's thoughts. Eventually whoever finally gains the wisdom of the things around him will achieve Nirvana and will no longer exist physically but will stay like one of God's angels without ever suffering again.

Ch 24

This week I went to the biggest Baptist church in our little town. But it was for a different kind of service. It was for the funeral of a great man. It may not be appropriate for me to include it in this book but men like Clyde are the ones the rest of us should learn from. And it might give us a chance to cover some topics that we may not be able to cover otherwise. I barely got to know Clyde because I blew the chance by getting locked up. When I got out of prison, he was having health trouble and I took over for him by working for his wonderful wife in their yard while he was trying to get better. If I had spent my time behaving, like I'm trying to do now, I would have known him much better. All it took was a few months to learn what kind of man Clyde was. Being the brightest spot in someone's life gives you a reason to shine!

You can tell a lot from a man's workshop. I worked really hard getting his yard ready for him so that when he came home from the hospital he could enjoy it for a few more years. His shop had the awards he had received from work and a very large fishing lure collection. He had every kind of tool you would ever need, and a giant collection of unique items.

It is a great honor to be trusted enough for someone not to worry about you bothering any of their stuff. Earning someone's trust is a trait that is rare in many groups these days and it is something that everyone should try to achieve. Trust is something that can't be forced and it takes a long time to get—but just a second to lose. Trust and honesty are probably the most important things in life. If you ever get to that point of earning someone's trust, you should be very proud of yourself and never let them down. Doing this isn't a high-profile action that everyone will notice, but it is a value that you will profit from in the long run.

The pastor today spoke of this man's decades of work teaching the children at their Sunday school and his dedication to the Lions Club and their camp for kids. Clyde was voted Humanitarian of the Year. Clyde was interested in many things and how they worked.

There are so many interesting things in our universe that one can't help but wonder about how they came to be. Scientists have created what they think is a new form of matter that they are calling Fermionic gas. They used about a half million Potassium atoms that they chilled to absolute zero (-273° C) which is as cold as we can get things. They don't know exactly what they will be able to use it for, but it will probably be used in quantum mechanics for matter that behaves in waves instead of individual particles. How smart do you think someone would have to be to create that? How smart do you think someone would have to be to create the potassium atoms that the scientists used? Many people think that a supreme being, or God, created everything—and it is unimaginable for us to consider this or doubt this one way or the other. It is just simply beyond our grasp and that is probably what we need to realize. Faith is when you believe in things that you don't completely understand. Even if we figured out everything in this universe, and then we went out to the farthermost point that any scientist knows about, what would be on the other side of that? None of us will ever know the answer to that, at least not while we are on this planet Earth.

It is just best for us to be happy in our bodies and to enjoy the things that we have instead of trying so hard to get more stuff. If you go to prison, you lose everything, and you learn how nice the old stuff was that you once had. It's easier to understand that God is all you need when God is all you have! Wasting the time we spend on Earth trying to get more stuff or make others happy could be one of the biggest mistakes we make. Enjoying the wonders of the world is something that almost anyone can do, and it is something that almost everyone takes for granted. We should value our precious time on Earth and teach others to do the same.

Ch 25

On this beautiful October Sunday morning I set out for the closest church because I have a last minute birthday party to put together this afternoon. It's for a 55-year-old friend of mine. He's actually a good friend of another good friend of mine—and the father of a little girl I wanted to be my stepdaughter. My good friend is her godfather in case anything happens to her dad, so we are all kind of like a family. So, if you are not confused yet, you may be in the next paragraph.

I was on my way to a church in which the newspaper showed the church service was 10:00 a.m. and their sign in front says 10:00 a.m. But a large banner says 2:30 p.m. When I got there at 10:00, nobody was there. So I made a mental note of this and figured I could go to the 2:30 service some other day if I needed to in order to accomplish my mission of a church every week.

As soon as I left, there were motorcyclists behind me which reminded me of our ride yesterday with "the birthday boy." Luckily around here there is a church every few miles. In just a few blocks, as I pulled in to let the bikes go by and try to figure out what to do, I was at a church!

Their service started at 10:00, and I had been to this type of church already but I didn't have time to do much of anything else so I went in. They sing, but they don't have any instruments. This was a much smaller group than the other church I went to like this one, and I was really noticed by the regulars. I was surprised that the sermon started out just like the one I had heard a couple of weeks ago. Maybe all the pastors have a program they can follow if they want to. It was about Adam and Eve and the apple and when they realized they were naked. But the nakedness this might symbolize is the nakedness a Christian would feel without their faith. Once you have given your life to the Christian way of life, you feel naked if you slip and do something that is not Christ-like. I know I feel much better when I stick to my pure way of living.

However, I cannot turn my back on my friends, and I must be strong and show them that Jesus has the best plan for our lives. I know I may slip occasionally, but I'll bet it doesn't happen very often. And if it does, I already know I have everything I need to be happy in life so I will just have to slow down and regroup.

Everyday is what you make of it, and others will always try to interfere with your happiness with their selfish needs and wants if you let them. Slow down and enjoy the simple rhythm of your heartbeat. Everything you need, you already have. Your mind and body will then allow you to get everything else if you try—everything that a Higher Power allows us to dream up, complete or invent. But just as easily as it was created, it can be destroyed and we must stay prepared to start over from nothing at any time. *Good* is very simple compared with *Evil*. Satan will try to make you ignore good things and be attracted to bad things. He will try to slowly whittle away at your happiness until you are weak and then he will welcome you through his open door. Self-indulgence is his lifeblood. Humility and gratefulness are his greatest fears. Early on is the best time to defeat him. If you give him nothing to work with, he is defeated before he even gets started. Once he has you, you must return to your beginning and relearn what really makes you happy. Satan's gate will always be open. Close the gate and be happy with yourself.

Ch 26

Well this is always my favorite part of writing this book—starting a new chapter! I just got back from another new church! I had considered skipping a weekend so I am really happy now that I made it to another one. I usually get a good message from every church and this week was no exception.

I had planned on going to a different church from the one where I ended up. Since I got out of prison, I have been doing house and yard work—but then I finally started up my business again. When my first totally new customer came by for some work, I told them about the book I was writing and that I would visit their church. But when I called them this morning, I wasn't able to reach them so I guess I waited too late to make that plan happen. I was running out of time to come up with a new church. But, on the way to my other house and shop, I pass a carpet store and noticed on their big sign are the letters "CHURCH 10:00 a.m."—so with no other plans, I decided to see if they really had church there, with a backup plan of another Baptist church down the street past them. Sure enough they had chairs set up in the front office section and a Peavey speaker system. The karaoke system played some inspirational music and the preacher's wife sang along and she was very good! The words to the songs were projected on the wall so we could try to sing along if we wanted to.

There weren't very many people—only ten total, but we sang and I held up my hands in praise for the first time. I needed to hold up my hands because I had felt a little bit down earlier this morning. Running with my old friends has my recovery at a turning point, and I have to make some important decisions—but back to the church.

The preacher talked about how complacent we get when everything is going good in our lives. We can go to church every week and thank God for all we have but still not do anything to bring someone else to the Christian way of life. Going to church may satisfy someone's thoughts that they have done enough. They have done more than if they had not gone to church at all. But by the next week, they will feel totally empty and will go to church for another few dollars worth of spiritual gas. When you are living and truly projecting God's way of life, you will be giving energy to everyone you meet all day and all week. By Sunday you won't be dragging to church but your own personal wind will blow you in the door!

Today the preacher spoke about Isaiah and how he told the people that with God even the most unfortunate life will become a success. Isaiah lived in Judah during the 8th Century before Christ. Judah was in the "southern kingdom" and even though they were threatened by the mighty power of Assyria, their main problem was their own sin. That is still our biggest problem today. People who drink and drug aren't always lazy but they are always lost. Many times they are just looking for something to be a part of. They see so many people living in sin that it just seems normal. Then to make matters worse the successful people in our society want to hate and condemn them rather than help them. The lucky ones think they are so much better than others. If you are successful and you think you are "so right," take another look! It's dangerous ground to walk on with your presumption of dominance. You feel so sure of yourself in your evil. Your wisdom and knowledge led you astray and you think no one will notice. How arrogant to think you are better than another human being. Is it easier for you to turn your back and enjoy your own prosperity, pretending nothing's wrong while others suffer? The "lost people" get nothing but hate from the lucky ones, compounding their misery and enforcing their need to rebel. Many turn to crime and the addicts risk everything for just a moment of drug-induced pleasure. How many people need to be locked up to avoid dealing with the real problem? Isaiah 28:20 – The bed is too short and the covers too narrow, just like prison! Isaiah 61:1 – The Lord has filled me with his spirit and has chosen me to bring good news to the needy, to heal the brokenhearted, to open the prison and release those who are being held captive without just cause.

Ch 27

This Sunday my Mom and I went to the "city" to a type of Protestant church designed by a German monk named Martin Luther. It was sort of like the church we are members of and sort of like a Catholic Church. They said today is the 18th Sunday after Pentecost. So I looked up some information about Pentecost. It is like the beginning of these types of churches. It's also called Whitsunday and it starts 50 days after Easter. Easter celebrates the resurrection of Christ. Pentecost was a feast where Jews and early Christians celebrated. Many spoke different languages but somehow they could understand each other. Many of the people were different looking but they saw this as interesting instead of acting with fear or with the hate that different types of people show each other today.

In this church, it looks like they believe the Bible is errorless and there's one God but three parts or persons—Father, Son, and Holy Spirit. They believe that God created everything. Adam and Eve are everyone's "first parents" and they brought sin into the world. So now we are born in sin, and to live without a relationship with God is further sin. They believe that Jesus is the Savior and to believe in him will make him our savior. Only belief in Jesus can save us from God's punishment. Jesus will come for his believers. Even the dead believers will also be raised to eternal life with Jesus. Believers are required to spend most of their time teaching others about Jesus and eternal life.

This type of church would like you to consider families staying together without divorce. During the service they pause for silence and self-examination. They tell you that self-examination on a regular basis would be a very good thing. I believe this too because I see my own recovery beginning to slip. Next, the children went up and sat on the steps by the pulpit with the pastor. He asked if any of them had done anything wrong this week. Some heads shook "yes" and some shook "no." He asked them if they can talk to God when they have been bad and they all looked at each other. The pastor told them, "That may be the best time to talk to God." Like all of us, they will probably need to be told that a few more times in their lives.

But the strangest thing is that the main sermon and the sermons from some other churches have all been about the same part of the Bible. Lately several pastors have preached about Genesis. They talked about when Eve was made from Adam's rib and the "apple" story and some about marriage. I can see different churches covering the same topic on the same weekend, but to go to three entirely different churches on three different weekends and get the same story is uncanny at best. I guess God wanted me to hear this lesson and for it to sink in. Genesis is a story that peaks your imagination. It portrays all kinds of events that could be very hard to believe. But then on the other hand, who could have made up a story as wild as this. I wonder if God had already made the universe and then made Earth. Or did he make them both during this creation story? He must have felt good if he created all of this in such a short period of time. But His feelings are supposed to be impossible for us to comprehend.

God gave this woman to man to be his helpmate. Somewhere along the line the "helpmate" just became the "mate." I personally have gotten nothing but trouble out of all my mates. I haven't totally given up hope because I know the dope didn't help matters. I know a religious woman would be more faithful. Maybe God wants us to meet a few wrong people before meeting "the right person" so we'll know how to be grateful for the gift. I see some good marriages where the two realize that it's a give and take relationship on both sides. Marriage isn't a fantasy and the new quickly wears off. Then it becomes work. But like all work, a marriage can be very rewarding. If you are young and you're obviously reading this, please don't have sex or get married to the first happy relationship that comes along. But if you do have sex, make sure you have decided to get and stay married. And since you are probably not ready to give up some of your freedom, I would suggest that you wait until your late 20's or even 30's. We were meant to be in a man/woman relationship from the beginning, and one of the rewards is your children who are made in your image.

We were made in God's image. That is why no matter what we say or do, deep down inside, we all know right from wrong. There are many types of "apples" that God still tests us with. Sometimes we slip and if we don't catch ourselves, we fall all the way down the hill. The bottom of my hill was prison, but I hope you don't roll that far.

God rested on the seventh day. ("*God blessed the seventh day and made it holy.*" Genesis 2:3), but it was such a long time ago and so many calendars have been made since then, I don't think any of us know which day—Saturday or Sunday—is truly the Sabbath. I think if you observe either one and follow the path of goodness, then you will be accepted in the afterlife. The Lord is merciful and he wants you to come back to him. You only have one chance at life and now the future is more important than the past.

Ch 28

Well miracles do happen! I got my "running buddies" and their kids to go to church! I met a man at a job site earlier this week, and I told him that I was writing this book and he told me about his church. But he didn't tell me he was the pastor! He did tell me about his motorcycles and his wife's motorcycle and that his church welcomes bikers. I think it was a miracle that I was able to get my friends up on a Sunday morning after they had stayed up almost all night. When I first got to their house, I never thought the whole group would make it. They were going to ride the bikes—but it was a little cool so all six of us piled into my truck. It is probably the farthest trip to a church yet, and I thought we would be late but I figured it was better to be late than for this group never to get started going back to church.

When we finally got there they began with everyone shaking hands and even some hugs. Then after the service started, they had another break where everyone walked around greeting each other. And I don't mean just the people sitting near you, but almost everyone there made it around to see everyone else. Then we sang some songs, which I thought would totally bore the kids. But they obviously had been to church before with somebody and they took it all in stride. I was real proud of them.

Sometimes it is just uncanny how appropriate the sermons are when you make it to church. The pastor preached about kids and their parents and about how important it is to train them while they are young. He talked about how he has been on trips to poorer countries and has seen children act better than most of the spoiled brats do in America. He talked about stern punishment and how the Bible tells us to discipline our kids.

When they are between the ages of approximately three and twelve, you must be firm with them without crossing the line and hurting them. Without any discipline they will run wild. Before the age of three, they are just babies and love is the most important thing to show them. However, after twelve, it is too late! They have already formed their roots and will only rebel. By the time they are teenagers, we better hope that their parents/guardians have spent enough time with them—or they will just have to learn for themselves the hard way.

Large businesses and industries owe it to this country—the country that made them successful—to spend more of their profits designing back-up plans to catch the children who "fall between the cracks." At a certain point in a young person's life, it becomes obvious that they are lost. They are not comfortable in the situation they are in and if they are not given any options, they are easy prey for gangs. Most kids like something—even though it may not be school work. Instead of quitting school and hitting the streets, there should be programs where they can work at something that they are interested in and get a G.E.D. at the same time.

The breakdown of the family has led to kids learning how to act from what they see on television. Kids today watch too much television and play a lot of video games. But in the future, video games will redefine our children's education. Learning institutions can capitalize on the possibilities that videos provide. If you can get their attention, then you can teach them. By using programs that are similar to their favorite games, you can teach job skills that employers are looking for. Then, when they get out of school, they will be able to join the work force.

Separating fantasy from reality has become a problem for most of America. Many people think that what they see on the news or in music videos is all that life has to offer. The good life is too boring to be reported or made into a video. Some are lucky enough to stay out of prison in their early years—only to find trouble later in life. We finally learn valuable lessons but by then our lives are almost over. The crimes that young people get involved in are no one's fault but our own. We let our schools become a breeding ground for immoral behavior. When the "bad" kids interrupt the learning process, the whole school suffers. It's a downward spiral that starts with marriages that break down due to wandering eyes and minds. Not enough chores and church will teach kids the wrong lessons. We, as adults, think that little moral slips aren't that bad and by themselves they may not be. But when enough people slip, all of these slips are then multiplied by all of the families in your area. Then the lack of values affects fragile minds while they are at school and can multiply even more. Then we end up with kids not learning what they need in order to be successful in life. Instead they are learning on the streets with the other "bad" kids who have learned the hard way to take advantage of "the new guys." The new kids think that this life looks like fun, and they are put to work doing the things that are the most dangerous. Eventually it becomes "the only way" and a question of survival. All of this could have been avoided by parents living like Jesus has taught us.

Wild glamorous lives look like fun in the movies and on television—but when the show is over, the actors can take off their makeup and go home. Trying to live that way in real life will only cause you trouble. If you think you'll like prison, you're wrong. It's a one-way trap door and it will be too late to change your mind after you're there and going home will not be an option!

✎Ch 29✎

Well it's a sad day for me. I lost the last twelve chapters of this book because of a computer problem. So I have to start over from my notes. I hope you have enjoyed what you've read so far, but I'll bet the first time I wrote them they were better. I felt like quitting and crying and all of that stuff—but what good would that do? It's times like this that being able to talk to Jesus helps. I hope all of you have a higher power to see you through the tough times that life throws at you. I must continue to focus on all of the good things in my life. I am lucky that I am able to work on this book at all since I could have very easily still been locked up.

It is Tuesday evening now. We have tried everything and everybody we could find to unlock this "corrupt" file. I was half way through with this book and I lost about half of what I'd written. So I will try to rewrite from memory everything that I lost.

Now I'll tell you about this week's church outing. This weekend my good friend and his family went with me to a church that I knew I would include in this book before it was over. They started it about ten years ago. It is out by the big lake where we partied for years. I watched this little church grow and grow. I knew of several people who had quit drugs and had visited this church. A man who came to visit us in one of the prisons where I was locked up goes to this church. He's a Christian Biker and his group is allowed to visit prisons. My friends who went with me today are alcoholics. They drink everyday. I love them and their little boy is like my nephew. His wife went with us but she stayed in the bathroom most of the time. Sometimes she carries beer in her purse. If you can't go without beer for two weeks, then you have a problem. I never could before I got locked up.

Prison is a good rehab, but it forces you to quit. When you get out, you have to find something to replace the void that you once filled with your drug of choice. And if you ever do have a slip, then it is more important than ever to get on top of this problem before you ruin your life. I still have to work at it ever so often.

Like most topics, the internet can offer you rehab information which you may have to use. Wow, I'm looking at it now and some of the pictures look like the places where movie stars must go. Some of them give you drugs to make you not want the other drugs—and I guess if that's what it takes, you can try it but I don't suggest going that way. The cravings usually never go away because they always remain in your memory and if you don't redirect your life, eventually you'll succumb to that craving. If you do, it's not the end of the world—but a "slap in the face" that should make you try harder.

As a long-time addict, I suggest that you just stay away from the "party" crowd (the heavy drinkers or recreational drug users). It is hard to stay away from some of your old friends. Not many people are strong enough to be around alcohol or dope without using if they have used it in the past. I get those feelings some times. But if I make myself get involved in one of my projects, the day is soon over. I can then enjoy a good dinner and after that I exercise a little while I watch TV.

Feeling good the next morning is your reward, and I always think about what I'd be doing if I was still in prison. When I was in prison, I didn't think I would ever watch TV again. I thought of so many projects to do that I would never be able to slow down long enough to watch TV. One of those projects was this book. I have several more projects dreamed up but right now I am enjoying being with my Mom, writing this book, and living the good life. One day I will be through with this book and return to "the world." That's what we called society in prison, "the world." I'll be "out and about" and working on those other projects. At that point, it will be more important than ever to pay attention to my sobriety. No short-term high is worth risking being confined and told what to do. Remembering that every minute is what it takes to stay straight and stay out.

∞Ch 30∞

The good news today is that we found a computer program called "Can Opener" to recover some of the stories I had written! The bad news is that it is all mixed up and I have to sort it out and rewrite it. I am glad my mom worked so hard on this because otherwise I don't think I would have been able to complete this book on time. And there were stories I had written that I would not have remembered; they would have been lost forever. I'll have to spend the next few months sorting all of the "sentences" and putting them back in order. WHAT A MESS!

This week we went to church at a school. It's hard to believe that but we did. You know, with the old separation between "church and state." But out here where we live the churches rule! And that is the way it should be. I love going to church now! I have been to a lot of churches in the past several months, and I enjoy the fact that all of them are a little different. I am beginning to think that the key to spiritual happiness is to be open to many different religions and churches and their way of living with their Higher Power.

Higher Power! Higher Power! That may be what we all need. What do you think? Do you have any suggestions on how we could all live in peace and happiness? If you did, would you stay quiet or would you let someone know how you feel? I am letting everyone know exactly how I feel. However I do not claim to be right about any of this. I will always be a student. But I am absolutely sure that we all can use a force of some type to keep us powered in a direction that benefits our life on Earth.

Today was the opening day of deer-hunting season, and the preacher dressed in and spoke about "camouflage!" He talked about how we tend to blend in with our surroundings. Even Christians who believe strongly in their faith have a tendency to blend in. Satan, the devil, or whatever you want to call him, wants us to hold back in our representation of Jesus. Are believers afraid of what others will think if they are obvious in their Jesus-based way of life? Or, are we just lazy with his teachings? We know that Jesus wants us to stand out and speak his message but we often have the tendency to act lazy in our faith. Some Christians are somewhat afraid of what nonbelievers might think about us. Some are afraid that it might cost them financial loss with a business venture. I say to you right now that we should never be afraid of anything, especially our faith in Jesus. No one will ever think less of you for displaying your trust in your own personal higher power. They may look at you funny or they could dislike you already. So don't worry about what other people think. You should worry about your own faith. Your own faith will give you your own personal strength to conquer any situation that you will encounter in your life. Your own personal strength is what you need to obtain your own personal happiness.

The preacher used his message with his camouflage. Now it's my turn to use the natural camouflage that God put in our world. Many of us look at nature but don't see it. Like so many things we use or see everyday—you don't really notice them. If someone could slap you and make you notice all of the things that you are missing, would you mind? Let's talk about one of the things we don't think about much. It's one of the easiest to get to and one of the most abundant. God or some incredibly smart person, or an extremely lucky alien scientist, has developed over 350,000 different types of "plants." They are part of the system that was developed to keep animals alive. It's hard to imagine that all of these plants were created by accident. Most plants are *autotrophs* which need sunlight so they can make their own "food" or energy. Working with and studying plants can keep you from using drugs. Anything that is interesting enough to keep you occupied will help keep an addict clean.

Plants consist of green algae, land plants, non-vascular plants, vascular plants, and seed plants. There is not a botanical word vegetable but it is considered the fruit on a plant. One type of non-vascular plant is what we call "moss." Bryophyta (moss) grows close together in damp shady locations. There is not much if any separation between the stem and leaves. Most of their lives they only have one set of chromosomes until their reproduction cycle. A microscope is an inexpensive way to enjoy the 10,000 different types which are small but very beautiful.

Vascular plants have special tissue to transfer moisture. A fern is one of the simplest vascular plants and there are over 19,000 different types. A fern has leaves but no seeds. Then you have what is most people's favorite—flowering plants, which you could spend years studying. And possibly the most amazing are trees. Whoever gave us trees must have really been planning ahead in order for the power tool business to survive!

So whether you believe that God created everything or not, it is hard to imagine how it all came together and where it's all headed. One thing for sure—it is too special to waste it by being drunk or high.

Ch 31

This week I went to a church on a creek. Well maybe it was on a creek when it first got started and back when it got named around 1900. Now it's by the highway with a big auditorium in the back. I went by to get my friends this morning, but they must have still been asleep so I went by myself. We always pass this church on our way to the city, and I would tell my mom, "Someday I will go to that church." So today was that day!

We stood up most of the time and I was ready to be an old person so I could justify sitting down like they were. Then at one point they had the visitors only sit down, and almost everyone came around and stood in line to meet me! So if you're shy, this is not the church for you. Outside of that it was very relaxed and upbeat with some young people playing praise music in a group that sort of sounded like a rock band. They were so good, I almost couldn't believe it. I was surprised that the place wasn't packed just to listen to them. There were more teenagers and "twenty something's" at this church than older people. It was probably too loud for old people. The "kids" would jump up and down and run up to the stage to bow down and pray.

The preacher's sermon was about HOPE, and how important it is. So I got the dictionary and looked up "hope"—which means "something that you long for." Hope in Hebrew is Tiquvah and means "a cord and/or something that you long for." Many people's lives and hopes are hanging by a thread. Qavah in Hebrew means "to bind together and/or to patiently wait." When many cords are combined, it increases strength. Many people bound together will be stronger and can accomplish great tasks if they are also patient and work together.

Romans 5:2 says "Rejoice in the hope of the glory of God." I personally think that our lives should be at a point where we can do more than hope for God. You either feel worthy of God's glory or you don't. If you don't, you should work on changing your life to a point where you can feel glorious about yourself. People who have never been confined should be grateful that they haven't. Sometimes it isn't easy to realize how good you have it. I know prison will give you great appreciation of your freedom. When you get your freedom, you tend to thank the Lord for it. And if you don't, you will probably be headed back to prison. Isaiah 43:18 tells us "To forget the former things. Do not dwell in the past."

Many people want to get out of prison and forget all about it. I know that if your past is bad, then you should repent and start over and not let it keep you from moving on to a good life. But I personally think that remembering some of your bad times can keep you from returning to them. I guess it just depends on the situation. Knowing when "*too much fun*" is *too much* is a good time to remember a bad time. Whether you have been there or not, thinking about what prison is like may keep you free.

A story about "The Day of the Lord" says he shall pour out spirit on everyone and those who believe will drink his word. Old people will dream and the young will see visions. At this time there will be so much bloodshed that the moon will turn red. On this great—yet terrible—day, many people will finally ask to be saved. On this day the judges will be judged. He will punish the officials who punished His children unjustly. Fire and clouds of smoke will darken the sun. Those who know of their own wickedness shall burn; those with nothing will emit great joy, and those who have created suffering shall suffer tenfold. Those who have obeyed the teachings of Moses shall be as free and happy as calves that have just been released from their stalls.

Ch 32

Well they say it's the harvest season so this week I went to a church with Harvest in their name. Actually I needed to go to a church nearby and this one met both needs. I needed to get back and work on this book all day. I didn't think I would even go to this particular church since it is one of the most common types of religions, and I have already been to at least one other like it. But you just never know what's going to happen when you wake up each day. Also I needed to do some yard work and burn tree limbs while it is so nice outside. Then I can watch the last NASCAR championship race while I work on this book! This sounds like a good plan to me, so I'll be back "in a minute!"

Well I'm back but it wasn't a minute or even an hour. It is almost 4:00 p.m. After church I started on the worst spot on my mom's four acres—an overgrown tree that is the farthest out on the property, near the highway. It was perfect looking for Halloween. The vines have overgrown the tree and if I had not cut them down, it would have killed the tree. Sometimes our lives get overgrown—we let everyone grab hold of our time until we can't breathe.

The preacher today talked about how "strangers" can devour your land. Isaiah 1:18 says, "Come now and let us reason together." We should work together but not ask too much of our friends. If we are not greedy, we will not overgrow our friends. We should not live alone even though sometimes it might seem like it would be easier. Isaiah talks about many moral values and some important ways to live. We all sin but we should strive to live a life we can be proud of. Isaiah 1:18 also says, "Though your sins are like scarlet, they shall be white as snow." Jesus gave his scarlet blood to wash away our sins. This happens when you accept Him and decide to live the way Jesus—and most people—would want you to live. Live an honest, simple, unselfish life, and you will be happier. Give thanks when you can and endure your hardships so that you value the better times in your life.

Thanksgiving is only four days away, and I hope you are not locked up. If you are, I hope you have come to peace with your fate and learned to enjoy your way of life the best way possible. Philippians 4:11, "I have learned, in whatever state I'm in, to be content." I believe that all of us will get another chance to prove ourselves worthy of heaven. I hope you have chosen a faith that will give you hope for your future.

I think of Thanksgiving as just being American, but similar festivals and feasts are celebrated all over the world. America's Thanksgiving is celebrated on the fourth Thursday in November. It was first celebrated in 1621 to thank God for a good harvest and to thank the Native Americans. A ship weighing 180 tons called the Mayflower left Plymouth, England in September of 1620 with about a hundred passengers. They spent weeks in the stormy Atlantic Ocean and on the way they devised the rules of how they would run their new colony. They missed their destination of Virginia and instead landed at what they called Plymouth Rock in Massachusetts. After a month off shore the scouts were ready to bring everyone in to land around present day Provincetown and they founded Plymouth Colony.

They had landed too far north and the bitter cold weather took the lives of half the group. Springtime finally arrived and the following year was filled with building homes and farming. They met the people who were already here and became good friends. They both taught each other many things. At the end of the season when they had harvested their crops, the elected governor of the English, William Bradford, declared a day of thanks towards God.

In Canada they celebrate Thanksgiving on the second Monday in October. The early colonists celebrated at different times depending on which colony they settled in.

In 1789, George Washington chose November 26th as Thanksgiving and he used this time to warn people of the power of governments which should be limited to provide for our safety and happiness. Different states continued to celebrate Thanksgiving at different times depending on their harvest.

A lady named Sarah Hale was probably the most responsible for getting Abraham Lincoln to make it a standard date in 1863. But the President also used this time to call on all Americans to pull together in unity. Then President Roosevelt moved Thanksgiving up a week in 1939, but two years later it was designated on the date it is today. Benjamin Franklin was mostly responsible for the “turkey” part. He wanted the turkey for our national symbol because of its beauty and value. But the eagle got that job, and the turkey got the ax.

Ch 33

The time has come for me to start going to churches that are farther away—some that I want to include in this book before I finish it, and I even have a full tank of gas this week! But Mom wants to go to the city and go Christmas shopping this afternoon so I guess I'll have to go to one closer.

During the week, while my friend and I were out driving around trying to make a buck, I saw a little chapel. A long time ago, I went there with my girlfriend and her daughter so I guess I'll go back and see how that church is doing. I'll "see you" as soon as I get back.

Well I made it! It wasn't as close as I thought but it wasn't that far away either. I met a lady who had already gone to the Catholic Church earlier in the morning and then she went here also. We had a good chat and I told her about this book. And I met a lady who lives across the street from another good friend of ours. So I guess the old saying "it's a small world" is true. I told the pastor's wife about my life, and she said they also had some family members go to prison over drugs. Them "danged ol' drugs" affect more people than we think!

The pastor came down from the pulpit and preached to us up close. He spoke about how important it is to have a purpose in life, and if you don't know what yours is, you better think long and hard—and decide. Without a purpose in life, you are bound to wander aimlessly through life and never enjoy the feeling of being a benefit to others. No "purpose" can happen to anyone but with many people the boredom can lead to alcohol and drug abuse. When you can stay busy with something you enjoy doing, you will be less likely to waste your time getting high on alcohol or drugs.

The preacher also spoke about how King Herod tried to kill all of the babies in Jerusalem because he was trying to kill Jesus. Today, there were baby twins at the service and it is impossible to imagine anyone killing babies. Even unborn babies would be such a treasure if they were allowed to be born. I love my friends' children, and I still haven't found out if a certain little girl is mine or not. I do wish that I could have raised her. I know that would have settled me down. I had waited my entire life for one of my own. Their words can be so special that they have a unique power.

Most of my girlfriends already had children. Kids can get on your nerves though. Sometimes they take a lot of patience and they take special leadership qualities from an adult in order to discipline them in a manner that will help them in the future. Lazy parents get lazy children. It is the parents' duty to teach children honor and respect. As with most things in life, the Bible also has lessons that can help you raise your children. Jesus says to bring the children to him for they belong in heaven. Bring them up in the training and instruction of the Lord. It is said that we are born with sin but children seem to start out innocent to me. So I guess they start out "little angels." They learn the bad stuff from us. If they stay away from drugs, our children can be our crowning glory when we get old. If you know someone who drinks or does drugs, you should not hate them. Real Christians do not hate and they lead by example. That is the time when they need your love more than ever. However you cannot enable them. They are blinded by the drugs. It is a battle that must be won from the inside. It takes compassion and some tricks of your own to make them realize that they are wasting their chance at enjoying this life.

Ch 34

I finally made it to a church I should have gone to six years ago! If I had, I probably wouldn't have gotten locked up. I was arrested a few times when I was younger and then I started in on my series of DWI's which are now listed as felonies. But as long as I was in the big city, probation was easier to get. When I moved to the country, I found out that they will even send you to prison for nonviolent crimes. I always worked hard and none of my so called friends thought that I would ever be sent to prison. But my arrest record wasn't helping matters, and I pushed my luck too far. Even good lawyers have a hard time getting you out when your probation is revoked and they deny you a bond. So it would be wise to remember that.

On Friday we drove a few hundred miles south to visit my family and deliver Christmas presents, and we just got back last night (Saturday night). So today I am tired and I barely feel like going to church anywhere. I'm living with my Mom, and I need to go check on my other house, which is in the next town down the road. Several years ago we bought a house "on the highway" so I could run my business. It ended up also being a party house, and it's eventually where I fell prey to "the needle." So I took this opportunity to go to a church that I used to pass by all the time. We'd zoom by "high as a kite," driving way too fast. We were always in a hurry to get nowhere. We'd always rush to get places only to sit around and wait. Come to think of it, prison is just like being nowhere, so I guess I finally got there.

So I stopped by my house and then headed down the little highway which crosses the big highway my shop is on. It was the first time I had been down this road in a long time and the little girl who may be mine lives on this road.

I finally got to the church and my emotions were high. I saw some of my old neighbors including the pastor who lives next door to my house/shop. We used to be pretty wild, and I had to make amends. I stayed wasted most of the time even before I got on "the needle." I hated "junkies" and I didn't fall for that demon until I was 44. I didn't want to lose my young girlfriend who loved the needle more than anything, and she said that I would understand her better if I tried it. Boy was that a mistake! Soon after that I didn't care about her, or my business, or myself. It wasn't very long after my "first bump" that I was headed back to prison for a little bit longer than I did the first time. I really don't want to go back and it is very hard to stay off of all drugs once you have done them for a while. I got the idea for this book while I was locked up. I figured it would help keep me out of prison and hopefully a few others too. I hope the drug addicts will slow down long enough to read it. And I hope the friends and families of drug addicts will learn enough about the problem to find help for them. It's not just *bad* people who are on drugs.

It was the "First Sunday of Advent", the fourth Sunday before Christmas day, which I think is the start of four weeks for us to evaluate our lives and to realize just how bad the world needs a Savior—a Savior to save us from this evil world that most of us have had some part in creating. When you see someone you don't like or watch shows where people behave badly, these are two examples of the ways even good people like you are neglecting the values the prophets have tried to teach us. Little mistakes like judging others or idolizing actors on provocative television shows can lead to many of our problems.

You had better be ready to "meet and greet" when you go to a new church and especially when you go to one of these smaller ones. Near the start of the service, the youth pastor had the kids on the steps and asked them what we should do for Jesus' birthday. One of them said, "Bake a cake!" Kids are so funny! Then the pastor talked about how there is still time this year to turn your life over to Jesus and how he could still return before the end of the year. He said if God is waiting for the right time, then we will have to wait too and for us to remember that a thousand years is like a day to Him.

Ch 35

Today I will travel two towns away. It's cold and it's getting harder to get motivated. Now that I'm getting toward the end of the book, the last several churches are going to be farther and farther away. So to get motivated, I'll start this chapter now and finish it when I get back!

I made it back! I saw several duck hunters on their way in from the lakes. I went to a famous type of church that starts with the letter "P"—sort of like president. I'm trying to keep the identity of the churches generic in case I get any information wrong. I knew they had some famous hospitals named after them, but that's all I knew about this religion. They were sort of like my church—the one my Mom goes to, and sort of like a Catholic one. However it was the first one I've seen where the pastor was a lady. At first I thought she was just a member since she was dressed casually. She was real nice and she dressed like a priest during the service. They started with organ music and everyone doing silent prayers. Then they lit the "Second Advent Candle" to celebrate the coming of Jesus—or maybe the second coming of Jesus. They mentioned a lot of Hebrew practices and at one time called the Lord as Adonai, "Ruler of the House of Israel."

Then the children went up front and the pastor spoke to them about perseverance. That's what I will need in order to finish this book. And she mentioned lost sheep and asked the kids what they would do if one of their sheep ran off. One little girl said she would wait for it to come back—which is what many of us do when we feel lost. But I think she wanted us to go look for it and when we feel lost, to seek Jesus. Don't just sit around and do nothing. Many of us feel lost at times and many are scared to go to church. Most don't think they are scared but they are fooling themselves. What they are scared of is "change." They are afraid that they might have to give up their "security blanket"—their vice or habits which they have had for so long. They would feel naked without them. I know for a fact that none of these churches will make you change. However, you may notice that what you are doing is wrong and feel guilty. This is normal and you shouldn't let it keep you from visiting churches until you find one that you like. I can tell you from experience that you will be welcomed as long as you're not a raving lunatic. And if you are a raving lunatic, they have places for you too. Your thoughts become your words, your words become your actions, your actions become your habits, your habits form your character, and your character controls your destiny.

They had a feast after service and at first I wasn't going to stay—but I did. Needless to say the food was real good, and I met some people who knew some people I know. Most of the churches send form letters to visitors thanking them for coming. A few have made more effort than that. The nice lady at this church sent me a form letter, but it also had a nice handwritten note on it wishing me a safe trip on my journey to all of "my churches."

Ch 36

First I want to remind you that I am "no expert" on anything so read at your own risk! Today was the first day of Hanukkah so I'll give you one guess where I went. Did you guess? Yes, I went to a synagogue for the Jewish section of this book. Christians and most people know that Jesus was Jewish but you may not know that Hanukkah celebrates everyone's fight for religious freedom. Of course we had to drive to the closest city to find a synagogue. When we got there we told them we were not Jewish and that we were just visiting. They gave me a "yammica" to put on, but it's spelled Yarmulke. It is like a beanie or skullcap. Yammica is actually a Yiddish name which comes from a combination of German and Hebrew. In Hebrew the cap is called a kippah. In ancient Rome servants were required to cover their heads. When Jews go to church, they cover their heads to show that they are servants of God.

When they started the service, it sounded to me like they were chanting. And I guess they were because they were singing in Hebrew. I think they could sing the entire Old Testament, and I think they covered most of Psalms and Deuteronomy in the four hours Mom and I were there. When they spoke English, the words I noticed the most were "loving kindness." I've heard that used a lot at several churches. They spoke of the importance of each and every day on Earth and a certain fear of heaven. What matters most in Judaic teaching is to show ethical conduct toward fellow human beings. This religion deserves an enormous amount of respect as it is one of the oldest still being practiced today. I discovered that Hanukkah, the Festival of Lights, is not as big a holiday for Jewish people as Christmas is to Christians. One of the biggest Jewish Holidays is in May or June (seven weeks after Passover). It is called Shavuot or The Feast of Weeks, and it represents "The Giving of the Law," celebrating when Moses gave them the Torah and the Ten Commandments around 3500 B.C. at Mt. Sinai in a part of Egypt wedged between Africa and Asia.

Alexander the Great conquered Syria, Egypt and Palestine, but he let everyone continue to practice their own religions. But when Antiochus IV came into power, he oppressed the Jews and desecrated their temple. The much smaller force of the Jewish Maccabees revolted and triumphed. They were led by the son of the high priest, Judah Maccabee. After their triumph, they decided to rededicate the temple in Jerusalem, but they only had enough oil for one day to burn in their Menorah. However, the oil burned for eight days and lasted long enough for more of their special oil to arrive. Now to celebrate this "miracle" they light a candle (which is called shammash) in the Menorah every night for eight nights. Because of the importance of the oil, they like to celebrate with lots of fried foods, one of which is a sufganiot (doughnut), and they sometimes play a dice game called Dreidel.

Taken from Deuteronomy 6:9, Jews put a Mezuzah on their doorpost to remind them of God's love and that they are supposed to live by 613 mitzvahs/commandments which are derived from the first five books of the Old Testament. Now when most of us read these books of the Bible, we will come up with much less than 613 rules that we should live by. But the number 613 has numerical significance in several ways to the Jewish faith and if you combine enough different versions, they will come to 613.

The Rambams are a set of principals that most Jews try to live by. Here are a few: (1) God is unique and eternal. (2) You only pray to God. (3) Moses was the greatest of all prophets and what the prophets said is true. (4) God knows your thoughts. (5) God will punish you if you're wicked and reward you if you are good. (6) The "moshiach/messiah" will be appointed to end all of the evil in our world. The Jewish version of the Christian messiah is different. Their savior will be a human descendant of King David, a great military leader and a righteous judge. (7) Death is not a tragedy and the dead will be resurrected. Some believe that it is possible to make it to heaven although you may need to be reincarnated several times to be good enough. Wicked people will be tormented in life by their own personal demons and are simply destroyed at death, never to exist again.

Now around the world there are many different types of Jewish followers. They range from ultra-Orthodox traditions to Jews who tolerate some modern ways of life. In some places, they blend in and do not try to change others. But in some parts of the world, they can cause just as much trouble for people who are different as any religious fanatic can. As long as time has been recorded, people have fought with each other. Maybe it's time for each one of us to decide when fighting or violence would be justified and when it would be better just to let different people be different.

Christmas

This week I must take some time off from my travels to return to the church where I started this adventure thirty-six weeks ago. Back to where I was baptized right after prison, just like I had planned during the years I was locked up. So far I have managed to stay on track with all of the churches with a few minor adjustments. Today is Sunday, Christmas Eve, and at my age, the most important thing will be spending this time with my mom. When you are on dope, your priorities are so screwed up that you would rather be with your friends who "party" than be with the ones who really love you the most. This year it will be different.

This will give us the chance to discuss the one most people call Jesus. The one that many people think was a prophet—or even God himself—coming to experience what life on this planet is really like. In Greek, He is called Jesous, and Christos means "the anointed one" so some people call Him "Jesus Christ." In Hebrew anointed one or leader translates to "messiah." Jesous in Hebrew is Yahoshua or in Arabic, Yeshua. Like all words, they are different in most languages. Another prophet said he should be called Immanuel which means "God with us."

There are many versions of this story and here is one. Most religions know Abraham and after about 40 generations came Joseph, a descendant of David, who lived in Nazareth, Galilee. Joseph was Mary's husband, and Mary gave birth to Jesus, but they called him Joshua. Joshua means "God Saves." But supposedly she was already pregnant before Joseph and Mary got together, but an angel told him to take care of her for she wasn't unfaithful. The angel told him that she was conceived of the "Holy Spirit" and told him what the baby should be named.

Several King Herods ruled the land during this time but with the "help" of the Romans who were the most powerful. Caesar Augustus decided that everyone would have to pay him a tax so Joseph and Mary left home to go pay their dues. This is why he was born in Bethlehem, Judea. Bethlehem means "city of bread." During the religious waiting period for new mothers, they traveled to the temple in Jerusalem, Palestine. Jerusalem is a very famous city which has been fought over and conquered by several religions. Somehow, rich wise men from far away heard about this baby being born. Their knowledge of ancient prophecy led them to Jerusalem and they proclaimed that he would be the "King of Kings."

The murderous King Herod felt threatened and wanted to kill everyone associated with Jesus. The Wise Men had to return to their countries by different routes in order to escape. Trying to eliminate Jesus, King Herod had all the males under the age of two put to death. But he was too late because the group with Joseph, Mary, and Jesus had been warned and they escaped to Egypt. After a while, they felt safe and went back to live in Nazareth, Galilee. A man in Galilee named John was well known for performing the Christian ritual of baptism. Many people went to this man and one day Jesus did too. When he baptized Jesus, witnesses say that the sun shined brighter on Jesus. They also heard a voice from the clouds say, "This is my son." That Spirit then led Jesus up into the mountains with no food for 40 days. Then he heard another voice say, "you are hungry and if you are the son of God, ask for these rocks to be turned into bread." Jesus responded saying that food was not as important as the way you live and we should work for our food. The spirit continued to tempt Jesus, and He didn't like this spirit. Jesus told the spirit that God's word is better than his and that he might as well leave.

Later on Jesus heard that John the Baptist had been put in prison in Galilee. On the way to Galilee, Jesus saw four fishermen and told them that if they went with Him, he would teach them to be "fishers of men." He would teach them how to gather crowds and show them how to enjoy their lives. Jesus traveled country to country teaching his principles. Many "miracle" stories were told of very sick people coming to him and leaving better. He told everyone that they should let their good deeds be seen but give the glory to God. Jesus spoke of several rules in order to be worthy to enter Heaven.

You cannot attack another without cause

for that shall be murder.

You shall not want someone else's spouse.

Marriage should be for life unless one is unfaithful.

Do not speak unholy and "Let your yes mean

yes, and your no mean no."

Do not be provoked by words.

It is not your job to judge others.

Show understanding to those who are different

and forgive those who hate you.

Let your treasure be in your heart for that is all

you're guaranteed until the end of your time on Earth.

Many of his "miracles" were performed in Chorazin near the Sea of Galilee. Several men followed Jesus everywhere, and they became his disciples. One time, when they were in a bad storm on the sea, the disciples said that Jesus spoke and calmed the sea. A few weeks later, he found Matthew who was a tax collector. Tax collectors were not well liked, and they lived wild, selfish lives. Jesus told Matthew to follow him and Matthew did. Jesus sat with the sinners and his followers were confused. He told them that he could not find the lost without looking. He told everyone that they should not love any person more than they love God for if they do their relationship will be full of arguments. If your household is divided, you will not prosper.

By now he had twelve disciples and he told them it was time for them to go teach. He told them not to be afraid for there is nothing that will not someday be known. Keep your faith until the end. John was still in prison and both he and Jesus condemned the area for their unholy ways. Many people would treat their bodies bad and the rich were the worst offenders. There were many religious rules and laws concerning the temples that these people would follow. But Jesus told them that God didn't make those rules and that their bodies were temples.

Now Jesus hadn't been able to save John yet, and on King Herod's birthday the women in the family plotted to have him killed. John had told King Herod's brother, Philip, it was wrong for him to be with Herodias. So Herodias had her daughter dance to please the King. The King was so happy that he told her she could have whatever she wanted. She asked for John's head. This made Jesus very sad and he left town. Many people followed him and during the journey, they saw him heal many people. One of them was so thankful that they gave Him a boat. One day there were lots of people and very little food. They had some fish and bread, and Jesus blessed the food and asked that it be enough to feed the multitude. Everyone came to eat—and somehow at the end of the day, they were all full. Jesus told his disciples to sail away while he went off by himself. He went up to the top of the mountain and prayed for a whole day. A storm came up and he knew his friends on the ship were in trouble. He went to them on the sea and when they saw Him they were scared. He asked Peter to have faith and to come to Him on the water. When the others saw this, they said that Jesus must be the Son of God.

It is also said that Jesus did many more amazing things but eventually He told His disciples that it was time for Him to suffer also. He told them that one of them would betray Him leading to His death. But He said on the third day, He would rise again. He told everyone that from now on, if they ever wanted to see Him again, they must care for the thirsty, the hungry, the sick, and those in prison. A poor woman put very expensive perfume on Jesus and his disciples asked her why she wasted the only valuable thing she had. Jesus told them that it was her way of showing her faith. Judas was paid thirty pieces of silver to betray Jesus and he started his plan. When they came for Jesus a fight broke out, but Jesus made them put away their swords. So He was taken to the governor, Pontius Pilate. The governor asked Him several questions, but Jesus new this was his destiny and he did not answer in order to save himself. It was at their annual celebration, The Feast of Passover, when Pilate always asked his people who they wanted released. They asked for Barabas, and they told Pilate to crucify Jesus. Pilate answered them by pouring water on his arms and told them that Jesus' blood was on their hands. Soon Judas began to feel bad for what he had done, so he hung himself. They treated Jesus just as bad as most prisoners are treated. They even put thorns around his head and nailed him to a cross. Two robbers were crucified with him, but Jesus was crucified just because people called Him "The King of the Jews." Many people and soldiers wondered why He was being put to death. Afterwards, the King had them guard his tomb because Jesus had predicted that he would rise again. But an earthquake came and scared everyone off except for both Mary's. They saw wonders from the sky come and move the huge stone that sealed His tomb. His body had disappeared, and they heard the spirit tell them to return to Galilee and gather His disciples. When they were all gathered, they heard Jesus' voice say, "I have returned to heaven to wait; go tell all nations to observe my teachings."

It is now Christmas morning! The dog was barking because mom went up the hill to the other garage to get the turkey from the refrigerator. It's still dark, but I think most of that is because it is cloudy and rainy. Our presents are under the tree but we haven't opened them. Today is supposed to be the day Jesus gets presents. I wonder what He would want. Peace on Earth, of course! But until that's more important to everyone than anything else, it probably won't happen. Every religion would have to make it their prime objective.

Jesus also asked us to feed the hungry. What I have noticed is churches gathering and buying food for anyone who comes and asks for it. But some of them are so fat that they should be disqualified. No wonder their kids are hungry; they ate it all! In the Bible in 2 Thessalonians 3 it tells us that anyone unwilling to work shall not eat. These "busybodies" should settle down and earn the bread they eat. If they have money for cigarettes and other bad habits then they should not abuse charity.

Another gift He would want is Forgiveness. Is there something or somebody you hate? Do you drive and say bad things toward other drivers? Do you know that all of that hate and anger is ruining your life and your Christianity? When you become at peace with yourself, you will be able to accept people who are not just like you. You will finally be happy and be able to forgive others without even thinking about it. Noise and other distractions will not make you mad because you will be happy to be alive. Eventually it will become automatic because you realize that it is stupid to let anything ruin your day.

Mom just said—"It's time to open presents, so I'll be back in a little while!"

Well I got a lot of different kinds of tools! Most of our money went to buy presents for other people and their kids. And also money for my dentist so I guess you can say I'm getting new teeth for Christmas! One of my friends from prison said they are on lockdown and haven't even been able to go to the prison store which they call "commissary." I sent a few of them money, but it doesn't help if they don't let you out of your cage.

Ch 37

It's 7:30 a.m. on News Year's Eve! Time for me to celebrate the upcoming year—the year this book will get finished and my last year on parole! I saw in the newspaper where a church is having a popular band play this morning so that sounds like a good place for us to go on this New Year's Eve morning. I'll see you when we get back from the city!

Well we made an 80-mile-round trip down to the city but it was a bit of a disappointment because the famous band which the newspaper had advertised was not there. But disappointments are a part of life and the key is to change gears and make the best of whatever you are doing. Believe me, this was much better than what I was doing last year!

The church was real nice and they had a large separate building just for the kids. It must have been their old main building because the big new modern building was in back. Even without the other band, the music was very good. They had five ladies singing, a man singing lead and playing keyboard, the pastor played steel guitar, a kid on drums, two regular electric guitar players and one bass. So we still got our music in!

The first man I met was black and there were lots of black people there compared to most of the churches I have been to lately. He had been going to this church for 15 years! I thought that was a long time, and I couldn't help thinking that if I had been doing that too, I wouldn't have been locked up like a zoo animal. (I was pretty wild!) Another lady we met had been going there for 21 years! We also met a real nice 91-year-old lady who had been to India a few times to evangelize the message of Jesus. The first time she went she was only 65. She told us she was walking with a little girl and saw posters with her picture on them. The little girl had to read them and she was surprised when she heard that she was the guest speaker. She has overcome several physical problems, but says that her body is just a vessel for God to do with what he wants. Like me, she goes to different churches and it was a coincidence that we were there at the same time. But I bet I have still been to more churches this year than she has—or maybe anyone else.

There are certain things about some churches I don't like—such as the preacher asking us to repeat or say certain words. Although sometimes it does help get the audience involved and wake them up. But I would rather listen to a good inspiring story—one that leaves you with your mouth wide open rather than being led and told what to say. But we are learning that there are churches for everyone and that there is no reason for you not to get out and visit—especially if you have kids. If you are not taking them to church, or letting them go to one where some of their friends go, then you are failing as a parent. You might be drinking or drugging too much or you might just read them the Bible at home, but kids need to enjoy the unity and values that a good church can teach them. Just because you don't want to go, or they don't want to go, is no excuse. One day your child may wind up in prison and if you are still alive, you will wish that you had focused more on what is right than what is easy.

When we got home, we made leftover turkey sandwiches, which I love. For our "stay-at-home safe" New Year's Eve, we bought some steaks from the butcher shop to cook on the grill tonight. I learned that even if you can reach it, you should always ask the person you are eating with to "pass the salt." It is an ancient symbol of friendship and alliance.

The church we went to today has what they call a "lock-in" where everyone brings games and snacks and other stuff, and they stay all night enjoying each other's company. That sounds like fun and someday maybe I'll help them. Remember, New Year's Eve is for rookies so whatever you do, don't be on the streets.

Ch 38

Good morning! Today is a wonderful Spring Day! When this weekend rolled around in sequence, I was so sick I couldn't go to church or anywhere. Maybe it was a virus or a bad food product. I had just taken my friend's boy to the hospital and on the way home, I started coughing over and over—so who knows. Anyway, I wanted you to know that I had to go to a church a few weeks after the one-year deadline because I got so sick that weekend I thought I was going to die. But if I did die, I am ready to see what's next! I wanted to keep everything as honest as the facts I have to work with allows me to—so read on and both of us will try to wrap up this book and get it into the hands of a person who might benefit from reading it. Keep in mind, and I'll remind you again, when you are finished, it is very important that you give or loan this book to someone you think may benefit from reading it. Like the old saying goes, "An idle mind is the devil's playground"—which means that kids who don't have something to keep them busy will be easy prey for dope dealers. And young adults who are on dope need to regroup and find something better to be interested in—preferably something they can also make a living at. And older adults who are still "partying" too much need to quit or slow down while they still have their health. Days without dope and alcohol are much better than days recovering from "partying" or days wasted looking for more dope. Life can be hard and life can be interesting. Either way the drugs and alcohol will suck your money away and leave you more and more depressed. Hey, I just realized that "evil" is right in the middle of the word "devil's." I'll write more when we get back from church.

Yesterday when we went to the store there were some kids, young people, teenagers or whatever you want to call them, handing out flyers for their church. That's the only "sign" I needed for a place to make up this hole in my 52-church plan. I figured if they wanted people to come to their church that much, I should give them my time and money. Mom went to her church early and then she went with me. There were the cutest little twin baby girls with their mom and grandmother in the pew in front of us. It was a little hard to concentrate on what the preacher was saying because one of them was always staring at me. Both of them were looking—but usually just one of them at a time. I was staring back and making funny faces so that didn't help either.

At this small country church, they sang a lot and they will sing a lot more tonight. They wanted us to come back but we worked in the yard again all day and then tonight, I'm making salmon patties for supper. They are having a fish fry next month and maybe we'll go back when they have that. Our church is having a fish fry next weekend just like they did last year. I had not been out very long when I went to that fish fry.

Last Saturday I rode my motorcycle to the real big city for a custom bike show. It was fun but I have to be careful "running" with those guys or I'll end up back in prison. I didn't get home until 10:30 at night! That's way past my bedtime. It was only the second week in a little over a year that I didn't go to church. So this weekend I stayed home, except for going to this church where it's safe and comfortable, and I feel much better than I did last Sunday after the "Big Ride!"

Ch 39

Well it's my birthday! This is the first one straight and sober since I was a kid. Every special day now is the first one straight. My life is half over but it feels like it's just beginning. It's sad to think about all of those years wasted trying to get as high as possible, and all of the "friends" I had who don't care anything about me now.

We went through each day chasing another party. At the end of the year, we had nothing to show for our hard work. And it was hard work driving all over town all day and all night trying to find more drugs. And somebody was always calling me needing help. I was very generous and when people needed something, I was everybody's friend.

Today we are going to the city to a fancy seafood place to celebrate my birthday. While we are there, we'll visit another church that meets on Saturdays. They follow the principles of a big religious organization but this group met in a normal size house. They also have a radio program based on being a winner from birth. They worry about all of the false prophets as we all should. I know some people who don't even go to church for that very reason but they read the Bible every day and they hate the hypocrisy of many so called Christians.

I was at a church last night and I really liked the preacher, but he tends to go to that "holier than thou" level that seems to be directly opposite of what he is actually saying. He says that we should only listen to God's word as he holds up one of the many versions of the Bible. If we should only listen to God, then why should we listen to him? I have learned to listen to everybody, but I still follow my own feelings that my gut tells me is right.

Once again, I like preachers who tell stories and let you decide for yourself what you should do. I don't think anyone likes to be told what to do. When the time is right, God will speak to you and you will know it. It will usually be during bad times because that's when he has your attention. During good times you tend to think you are in control. Don't get me wrong. Many people have grown up with their faith and have stayed out of trouble. But if they ever have hardships, that is when their faith will be tested.

Being in prison is like a "high" (or low) all it's own. It's a place that no matter how much money you have, you can't buy a ticket to go home once you're there. It's an experience like no other! Prison teaches you to be very careful. You don't dare drop anything important because if it breaks you can't rush out and buy another one. You can't bump into anybody or spill anything without risking a fight. Psalms 27:14 says, "To wait and be of good courage." COURAGE: "The state of mind or spirit to face hardship." The waiting is the part that makes you enjoy something once you get it. Wait bravely and confidently for Him for He is the giver of all good things.

Today's church thinks that their version of the scriptures is the "only way" and outside of that I think they are on the right track. They say the keys to a happy life lie within the scriptures and obeying them will lead to eternal life. They think most of the holidays, which many of us celebrate, are pagan worship. They don't like jewelry, fancy hair or fancy clothes. They say we shouldn't automatically like a person because they look good for it is then possible for them to abuse that power. Then they will be able to get you to work for them in ways that only benefit them. If the devil was going to try to get you to follow him, he would probably come at you in an appearance that would hypnotize you. Many beautiful people follow God, but beware of the possibility of beauty alone getting you to do things that you might not otherwise do.

Ch 40

I packed up some work clothes and took off this morning not knowing for sure where I was going. I took work clothes so I could go out to my other house after church. It is the first time the sun has been out in a while, and I needed to get outside for some fresh air. We have had wet, cold weather for over two weeks.

My friend called to say he won't make it again today. I had to change my plans because I had a church in mind that I wanted his son to go to. So I remembered another church I had planned on going to when I was locked up. It's on the highway that goes to the next little town south of here. I bet I have passed it a hundred times, and it's by the church on the creek I went to a couple of months ago. The only reason I might not have gone to this church like I had planned, is because I have already gone to three churches like it. It's sort of like the fancy Baptist church I went to when I was a kid. I always try to get to each church early so I can meet some people and look around. But when I got there today, the parking lot was packed. I thought I was late so I rushed on in. I met a guy in a wheelchair coming out of the building, and he told me the first service was almost over and the traditional service had not started. He told me it would be in another building, so we headed over that way, and he told me he didn't need any help. He was in a wheelchair because he had lost his leg seven months ago but I didn't ask how it happened.

It was the busiest place I have been to in a while. There were lots of families and not many people alone like me. But I knew I was on a mission, and I found a good seat right in the middle of everyone. The choir came in and we all stood and sang several songs. But the best singing was four men—a soprano, alto, tenor, and a bass. They were real good and it reminded me of something I had seen on television a long time ago. We also sang one of my favorite songs that we used to sing in the first prison I went to several years ago—the one about Jesus going from the cross to the grave and the grave to the sky. It gave me "goose bumps."

They had a fairly new preacher and he was real good. The message he gave sounded like one I would give. He told everybody that just coming to church and giving money is not what being a Christian is all about. He said that some people think the church "just happens" and that it is not their job to do anything. He said, "The church is about people not the beautiful building." He had everybody fill out a piece of paper (I didn't get one) and write down a good deed they would do for somebody this week. Now most of the people probably couldn't decide what to write, but it did make an impression on everybody.

This was a very "well-off" crowd. Their last fundraiser brought in over $50,000. They obviously weren't worried about the decision over an increase in the minimum wage. I'm not either, but maybe we should be. Maybe it will affect the economy more than we think. Poverty should be the responsibility of the church. If the government was really worried about poor people, they would quit taking taxes out of their pay checks or anywhere else. If companies have to pay their labor force more, they may not be able to hire as many people or they will have to raise their prices to stay in business. Most beginning workers have to be trained. Not many workers make minimum wage after a few months. If they start at a higher wage, they may not ever see a raise and may not feel their hard work is rewarded. That would mean less productivity in the long run. However most minimum wage workers are young and have few responsibilities. Many live in homes with incomes over $50,000 a year. Most poor people are that way because they don't or can't work at all—or they continue to have kids they can't afford to raise. Some poor people are content and don't mind letting the government take care of everything. But what will happen when there are more poor "content" people than there are tired hard-working people? What will the government be able to do with that situation?

Over half of our good Americans pay no income taxes at all. This means that they don't have to pay for any of the government programs and when they vote, they will always vote for the candidate who thinks we need to give more. If this continues, we will all be broke!

So let's change the subject to a more positive direction! To make yourself happier and your life easier, on days you don't have to go to work, try this. Only focus on one or two projects, starting with the hardest one—or the one you really don't want to do. Most things in life can wait but getting these "big" projects out of the way first will make the rest of your day seem easy. Doing these projects early in your day, when you are rested, will make them as enjoyable as possible. The most important thing in life is to enjoy every part of it. Rushing through your day is a "sure fire" way to be miserable. If something ever happens and you lose your freedom, you will realize that *everything* really can wait. "*Everything*" is still going on without you. It may be going differently, but everybody else is still going without YOU!

Ch 41

Once again I took off this morning not knowing for sure where I was going. My friend called last night and said that he would go to church with me today, but he sounded like he had a good buzz going so I wasn't too confident that he would make it. When I didn't hear from him by nine o'clock this morning, I almost told my mom she might as well go with me to one of the churches on my schedule.

But I decided to wake up my friend anyway. When I got there he was awake and he had turned on his computer to e-mail me that he was not going. But since I was there, he had no choice. He was sick with his hangover but he had to go with me since I was there. By this time we had run out of time to go to the city and to one of the churches that I had wanted to go to—so we headed to a church we had seen before that is a little closer.

On the way, a black man was stuck in the mud from trying to cross the highway through the grass. You'll see later why I point out that he was "black!" It would have been easy for us to keep going, but going to church wouldn't make much sense if we could pass a brother in need—especially since I was in my truck with tools and a tow rope and chains. I always carry tools and a floor jack, and I have stopped many times to help people in need. So we got him out of the mud, and he asked how much he owed us. I told him that he didn't owe us anything except to not be so "dumb" next time. We continued down the highway and stopped at a church we had passed several times during our travels for work.

When we went in, I was surprised that everyone was "black." That was good because several months ago, my friend had mentioned that he wanted to go to a "black" church. They were still having Bible School so we sat and listened. Then my friend had to go smoke before the main service started. They remembered to pray for all of the people who are locked up which I think is the first time I've heard that. The preacher talked about the days before he was saved and how our troubles will still be there the day after we drink or use drugs. He begged everyone and anyone to come forth and not leave the service if you felt sad and lost. My friend almost went up. Later he said he wanted to but his feet wouldn't move. I told him that I knew how he felt and not to worry because he's "getting closer."

The black people at this church and some others I've met lately have been very nice to me. In prison it was a different story. Almost everybody runs with people who are the same race as they are. When I came out of prison, I was more prejudiced than I was before I went in. I had a few black friends in my life but they didn't treat me any better than most of my white friends. Once again, I think the drugs had a lot to do with the dishonesty. It wasn't until prison that I was around more black people than white people. I had always said if you were falling off a cliff, you wouldn't care what color the hand was that reached out to save you—so why should it matter any other time. All through history people have been afraid of people who are different from them. In prison people are your friends as long as you can give them something. But the more you give, the more they want and eventually you can't give them anything, and they turn on you.

May you have enough happiness to make you sweet, and enough misfortune to make you strong, some sorrow to keep you humble, and enough hope to make you happy again.

Ch 42

Another week zipped by! I got some more dental work done. So now I can really smile when I finish this book. I also have an appointment to get a physical and some other tests to see what the 35 years of drinking and drugging has done to my "over-the-hill" body. I also noticed this morning that my hair is getting thinner. But enough depressing stuff.

It's Super Bowl Sunday! My mom has helped me so much in my life, and especially since I went to prison—so unlike past drunken football games that I barely remember, mom and I plan on making this "Our Super Bowl Sunday." Last night mom and I bought some chips, pretzels, hot dogs and chili for the game tonight. My friends let me down again on going to church which is just as well because now mom and I can go to the city to one of the churches I had planned on taking my friends' kids to. One weekend I had seen the crowd leaving, and I saw a lot of young people. Mom deserves my attention more than anybody else in the world anyway, but I have a feeling it will be a good church for young people, and I wanted to take the kids.

It is a sunny, cold day which is as good as it gets in February. We are going to a church of living hope. I had a Living Bible when I was a kid and it was easier to read so maybe this will be an easy-to-understand church.

We were gone for a few hours. The church program was a long one compared to most of the others I've attended. This one was from 10:00 to 12:15. The weather was so nice when we got back home, we went out and worked in the yard and burned some leaves and brush. We haven't eaten much today so we can enjoy our Super Bowl munchies. It's now 4:30 and the teams are already on the field for the kickoff in about an hour. Once again, this will be another big event that

I will enjoy sober for the first time. It's not easy watching the big game without beer, but I do know it's the right thing to do.

The church this weekend was one of my favorites. It will be hard to decide on just one favorite church after going to all of these. It was another very casual church with free coffee, doughnuts and homemade cookies. It was in an old plantation-style house that at one time was probably in the middle of a lot of land. Now it's right on the highway and a few years ago, it was a fancy seafood restaurant. The young people were dancing and jumping around praising the Lord, and I even saw a barefoot girl and lots of tennis shoes. They were planning a Valentine's party for the married people, but I think one for the single people would be better. I'm single and lonely, so I kept looking for single women, and I had a hard time concentrating on Jesus. At one time they had some leaders of the church gather in front and people could go up and get hugs and prayers. The kids went off for their church, and it must be upstairs because I could hear them romping around. A group from the church had just gotten back from South America where they built a church in a small city. They also took lots of clothes, hygiene items, and other supplies for the people.

The younger pastor had a good message about when you're "born again" and born to live like Jesus would want you to. He said that your Baptism is just the beginning and that the "born" part means you must continue to grow as a Christian. He referred to 1 John, Chapter 3, which tells us about how Jesus laid down his life for us and how we should show our love for Jesus with actions and not just words. And Luke 11:28 tells us that it is not enough to show up and hear the word of God, for we are only blessed when we obey the word of God. It's all about believing, whether it's in Jesus or yourself, your dedication will create faith and confidence.

Ch 43

Well it's only Saturday, but I feel I need to talk to someone so here goes. My almost perfect recovery began to have more problems this week. Then for punishment, I got real sick. I feel better today, but for the last few days I have been sort of sick. I didn't think I would make it to a church this week. But now I think I'll try to go to one of the confessional-type churches tomorrow which has an early service. After that I can go to the church where I was baptized 43 weeks ago because it is also the birthday celebration of the pastor, and it is the week everyone stays after the service for Fellowship Dinner.

But back to my "perfect life." I guess I'll have to quit visiting my good friend because I keep ending up in situations that I know I shouldn't be in. Jeopardizing my freedom is not something that I should take any chances with because it wouldn't be fair to my mom or even the little girl that might be my daughter. Plus I'm too old to get another chance as good as this to get my act together and enjoy life.

I also wanted to start this chapter early because it's another big sports weekend for me. I might have already mentioned this, but after prison I was sick of sports. In prison, it's "hoopin' and hollerin'" all day—everyday. They jump around like they had bet their life's savings on every game. The constant noise is torture that you will never forget. Some of them yell and celebrate no matter which team is winning. But this afternoon the best football players in the NFL will get together and more important for me—tonight NASCAR gets rolling again. It doesn't seem that long ago that I was writing about the final race. But time flies when you're having fun and now that I'm over my sickness, still free, and back on a safe positive track, I think I'll celebrate. I'll celebrate by doing something you can only dream about when you are in prison—go shopping! I'll see you tomorrow.

Now it's Sunday afternoon. I got ready a little earlier than normal and made it to the church around 9:00 a.m. Our mayor was a greeter who welcomes people and later he held one of the chalices during communion. I sat in the back row which I later discovered was for the choir. I wondered why everybody was looking at me funny! But a real nice lady helped me with the rituals and when we went to our knees, I felt I had a lot to pray for. I haven't been that bad but it doesn't take much to start you on a routine that leads back to prison. Recognizing this and making corrections is what many people need to do in order to stay out of prison. So that's what I'm trying to do!

This type of church starts with the letter "E" and I'll let you figure it out. And of course this one is named after one of the saints. The Father talked about the ancient city of Corinth and about how rich they were. Most of them thought that a few hedonistic years were worth an eternity in hell. They spent their money on every kind of pleasure that was available. This is just like many of us do today. We need more stuff and more food. We could live without half of what we have and feed every person in the world. But even the best Christians have a hard time giving away that much. Many of us have been in situations where we had to do without simple luxuries and we are afraid to return to that life so we hoard our money. But remember, Jesus said, "Blessed are the poor, for yours is the Kingdom of God." Read the rest in Luke 6 to find out how "the time is now" if you want to earn the Kingdom of God. Suffering is part of earning your way to Heaven. Will we wait one day too long?

Ch 44

Success! I made it to another church this week even though I sort of cheated. I wanted to get back home in time to write this and watch the Daytona 500, so I had to find a church close by that I had not been to already—and one that had services that ended a little earlier. I also have some things I want to discuss about immigration so I decided to go to the "Mexican" church. I didn't understand very much they were saying but they were real nice and helped me find the pages in La Biblia, songs, and other material. Mom and I are taking a Spanish class on Tuesday nights and if I went to this church every week, it would definitely help my Spanish. The kids stayed in church with the adults so it was a little noisy, but not as noisy as prison so it didn't bother me at all.

The weather is finally warming up and after church, the children seemed very happy. For some reason, the Mexican children seem happier than a lot of Caucasian children. I guess most white kids are just too spoiled to enjoy playing with sticks like these kids and like we played with when I was a kid. Before I start this next part, I want to say a special thank you to the many advocates across America and Mexico who work to protect the children who are victims of deportation.

Making money is important so that we can eat well and stay warm and dry. "E Pluribus Unum" is printed on the dollar bill and is Latin for "one out of many." Many different types of people came here and made this country. I know that a lot of the hard labor in America is being performed by Mexicans. Some are here legally and some are not. There are over 12 million illegal immigrants living in America, and they have three million American-born children. They are living here because it is easier and more fun for them than the life they would have in Mexico. It wouldn't be smart to send the parents back without their kids. And it wouldn't be "human" to send the kids to an impoverished life. Determining a good way of stopping illegal immigration is a topic we all should provide input on since it affects everyone. The only thing that makes sense is drawing a line now, setting policy, and enforcing it! All workers could be documented and made to pay higher taxes for a few years since paying higher taxes would still be better than the alternative of being returned to Mexico without a job. Shut down any business that pays an undocumented worker. After ten years of paying the higher income tax and no felony arrest, they could earn an American citizenship.

Good old Emma Lazarus and the Statue of Liberty says, "Send the homeless to me and I'll lift my lamp by my golden door." Since then millions have done just that by legally seeking what can be wonderful and exciting for those who are willing to work for a better life. There is no record of how many people come and try to live in America illegally, but a good guess is over a million a year. The U.S. Border Patrol's arrest figure rose to a high of about a million people back in 2005. Well maybe it wasn't really that many people because a lot of those arrests are the same people being arrested over and over. That takes a lot of manpower without providing worthwhile results. I don't know about you but that doesn't sound like a good use of taxpayer money to me, and my taxes are high enough already. The Justice Department said that some immigrants are rearrested as many as six times! Many of these are for violent felony crimes. It costs Americans almost one billion dollars to provide health care and incarceration for people "visiting" from Mexico and South America. There are enough "illegals" locked up in America right now to make a whole large city all by themselves. And what a wild city it would be!

So I think as long as people are working, they should be put into our tax system whether they are allowed to be Americans or not. People coming here to work is much better than having criminals and terrorists crossing our borders with the workers. Some people say they take jobs from Americans, and that may be true—but I think there are still plenty of jobs left for Americans who are willing to work hard. Fifty million Mexicans live in poverty and if the rich business elite in Mexico can't provide jobs for Mexicans, then their government should use their vast natural resources to provide incomes for their people so they aren't forced to go elsewhere for work.

Mexico has started a health insurance program for infants which is a move in the right direction. Children born in America should be born to Americans. Under the projected new law, the only way to become an American would be by being born to an American or a future American. Once again, if someone wants to be an American, there should be an easy process readily available that good people can use to earn an American citizenship. The U.S. Citizenship and Immigration Service needs more money to make this happen so they don't have to raise the application fee to a point that it is out of reach for most Mexicans. The U.S. spends millions on border security gadgets and cameras to watch the Mexicans come across the border, and we don't even know what to do with the pictures or the people in the pictures. Professional immigrant smugglers and their safe houses are the only ones benefiting from our so called increased border security.

America is very nice to foreigners. Voting laws provide foreign language to help them understand how to vote. Aliens seem to be able to get local driver's licenses and utility services which makes you wonder who is in charge of this country. Sensibly increasing enforcement to keep companies from hiring people who don't have approved American documentation would be the easiest way to get the illegal worker problem under control. Americans need to learn how to work together and come to agreements which solve problems quickly. Many new programs and categories for people who are already here have possibilities but lack long-term details like what happens when they are laid off or get too old to work. But if you make the system too difficult and complicated, it won't work. We need to make a simple working agreement that really benefits Americans. If you're an American then I'm sure you'll agree that Americans are the ones who need to benefit first of all. Then if the "illegals" don't want to comply with the immigration paperwork, and they are caught in America illegally, without any other crimes, they need to be put in a special "tent type" low-budget prison. Since most Mexicans are good workers, you then punish these "criminals" by making them work off fines by doing jobs that we usually send out to low-wage countries. These fines could then pay for them to be sent to Mexico City or other busy cities far away from our borders where they could try to find work. It will take decades for this situation to stabilize but having everyone documented and paying taxes is the only way—and the faster we deal with it, the better!

If you are not going to enforce a law, it should be removed from the books. Illegal is illegal, and eventually most criminals are caught up in "the system" where a good plan and laws can deal with them. And if a person isn't causing trouble, then leave them alone. Our prisons are full enough. If kids are making good grades and their parents are staying out of trouble, then leave them alone.

Slowing down the illegal flow of people across our borders will allow us to spend more money to totally secure both borders so that people who want to harm us can't come over—but the people we need for hard work can come over. Maybe if Mexico helped us with the border as much as Canada does, we wouldn't have this problem.

It's hard to tell parents they shouldn't try to get free schooling and health benefits for their kids if there is anything they can do to get it. But for Americans to pay for this, the parents need to be paying taxes and it would also help America if they weren't sending most of their income to their families in foreign countries. One proposal is to tax all monies wired to other countries. But our government sends more than anybody so that wouldn't work. Solving the immigration problem will take several different plans and several adjustments to these plans as problems and benefits are noticed. But immigration is not a problem without a solution. If the people we send to Washington can't solve our problems then why do we pay them so much money?

We may face much worse problems one day—and if we can't solve our immigration problem, then we will be in big trouble when real disaster hits.

Ch 45

Yesterday was as windy a day as I've ever seen in my life! The skies were red from the dust. Some states had tornadoes and some ladies I saw on the news said that God saved them. Well I guess God helped me survive yesterday, too, since my friend and I went to the city to shop for his son's birthday. I really like visiting the city and seeing all of the people, but I prefer living without neighbors that close.

My friend said he would go to church today but it will be a miracle if he makes it since he worked last night. We plan on going to the little church in the nearby town where our other friend lives. Both of these friends are always with each other and their kids are like brother and sister so we'll see if we can have a "family" outing.

Well I knew it would take a bigger miracle than being saved from a tornado if my friend made it to church today. So I used a backup plan and went to a church that's out in the other direction toward my house and shop. One day maybe we'll make it to that other church, but my year is almost up if it's going to make it in this book. Right now, I have churches planned for all of the remaining weeks.

This weekend's church is one that I heard about at my drug recovery class. A young lady was at the class with a friend of hers who just got out of prison, and this is where she said she goes. I didn't see her but I did see a few other people I knew from various places around town. I'm still surprised at how all of these churches get filled up. Watching the news it sounds like there aren't this many good people left in the world.

I pass this church's highway sign every time I go to my house/shop so I sort of knew where it was. But when I turned down the black-top road, it curved around so much I wasn't sure where I'd end up. But then over a hill I saw a steeple. Like most churches have done, they have added a new metal building but the main worship service was in their original church sanctuary.

I really liked the preacher and he was about the same age as I am. I don't know his background or if he's been through any life-altering experiences but I have a feeling he has. I like it when the pastors come down from the pulpit to preach, and he moved back and forth the whole time. During his sermon, he "talked" to some of the members in the pews which kept everyone awake and involved. He also had a sense of humor which made getting the message more fun.

This was another one of the most popular types of Christian churches and, like I have, he talked about how people get more excited about how they love a sports team or a hobby than they do about their love for Jesus. (If you are not a Christian, then you must still express your faith as being more important than anything else.) He also talked about how people are more concerned about what other people do than they are about themselves. If everyone would love and forgive the people who are not living a good moral life, then the Christian message would be more believable. When Christians get mad or judgmental, it sets a bad example so others have no reason to follow the Christian way of life.

America is a country founded by believers in God and in his son Jesus Christ. These believers have just as much freedom-based rights as nonbelievers, but sometimes those Christian ways cause them to be more passive than nonbelievers. Satan tests us every day and by doing nothing, you let the evil forces, which never sleep, grow stronger. We must realize that the battle is not with other religions, and it will take all of us to defeat some of the evil in this world.

Ch 46

Good Reminder Lesson: "You can't tell from the outside, what's on the inside." I took off right on time or maybe just a little early this morning! I wasn't sure where I was going, but, like other times, I was heading to the city on faith that my mission would be successful. I had a church in mind where I had seen a lot of cars one weekend while we were in the city.

It's now Sunday afternoon and now I see why there were still cars in this parking lot after I had visited other churches in the city. I got to this church early, and I had planned on a quick day and returning for a good roast beef lunch which my mom was cooking. But when I pulled up, I noticed that the service didn't start until 11:00 a.m., and that it was another "black" church.

The "devil" had me think for a second that I had enough black churches in this book, and I knew that the late service would throw me off my "quickie" schedule. I thought for a second about going to another church—or not going at all—but this is where God led me. So, I went in and it turned out great. They had a little book store with coffee and doughnuts, and I met a guy who used to be on dope and we had a real good talk. We talked about the Holy Spirit saving us from dope and keeping us off dope. I don't know about you, but I may never feel that my faith is that strong. I know that I live by everything that Jesus taught us—but I'm not sure if I'm totally saved yet. Maybe I'm just too humble to say that I'm totally saved.

I'm glad I was in a church, because in the past, being the only white guy isn't usually a good thing. But I didn't have a hard time getting noticed as a visitor and once again everybody was real nice. As a matter of fact this church, which was a community church and the largest type of religion in the "Bible Belt," was one of the most enjoyable churches I've been to yet. It was also the loudest with a real good organ player. A little woman with a great big beautiful singing voice started the service. The choir was behind her and we all clapped to the beat. This was a "fun" church with people moving around a lot, cell phones going off, and high fives flying. At one point, they had a "meet and greet" where everybody went around and told people what their favorite kind of cookie is. It was unusually different and a lot of fun.

The preacher was a little younger than I am and on average was younger than most pastors I've seen. He never stood still and he was a real leader with a "magnetic" personality. He worked up a sweat and came down to the people just the way I like. He said we should be ashamed for all of the different denominations of Christian churches. This division makes us weak and the devil stronger. He spoke about metaphors and images which many Christians think about—like dying and going up to heaven.

Depending on where you are on the planet, if we all went up, we would all be going in different directions. Going into the air or clouds are simply ways we try to explain things, and we should not interpret some of the things in the Bible literally. We are not supposed to understand God. However, we are supposed to listen to our inner voices when they first tell us not to do something. Everyone knows right from wrong, and our minds can trick us into making the wrong decisions so fast that we don't even realize it. When you first get that chance to make the *right* decision, you should quickly consider what the consequences could be if you make the *wrong* choice, and then force your mind and body into the direction that keeps you out of trouble—and one which would make God happy. In other words, when you have the chance, you had better run to Jesus. Christians are constantly learning how to walk with the Lord, and they must constantly work at how they treat their neighbors. We should always give all of the glory to God for anything and everything we have. Sports stars, actors, and musicians may be famous, but they should remember that they owe it all to God for the talents they use and someday these talents will be gone.

Ch 47

I survived the time change last night and I got up with plenty of time to get to the city for another church. I went to a "warehouse" church. Many of the newer churches these days are in large metal buildings that look like warehouses. It is a beautiful day that should make everyone glad to be free and alive. It's Spring Break around here and everybody must be out of town because there wasn't any traffic. I really enjoyed my ride—listening to a radio show that featured old classic rock and clips from TV shows that sang or talked about dancing.

This is a Christian Covenant Church and as soon as I walked in the door, I felt right at home. They had a great location because there is a huge park right across the street! They had more youth ministry groups than most churches, which were separated by closer ages. It was another very casual church with my old favorite—barefoot girls! Now that's relaxed! One guy had a "beanie" type knit cap on like I wore to keep warm when I was a kid. It wasn't cold but he kept it on the whole time. I guess it was his fashion statement—and lots of "old" worn out jeans that were probably brand new. Some people came in a little late and they looked like they had just come in off the lake. The Pearl and Peavey music equipment was top notch. When the guy in the band read us his message of the day, he didn't read it off paper; he read it off of an electronic device! So this was definitely a modern church which is good because young people need churches they can relate to. When they are young, they can be saved in more ways than one. Once you get on dope, it makes for a long trip—a trip I took personally and that I now want to *personally* try to prevent others from taking. Everyone who has ever had a problem with alcohol or dope can tell you what a waste of time it was.

The pastor talked about fathers and how children long for your smile—the same is true of mothers. Titus 2:6 says that young men should be sober-minded. Kids need our attention and patience—both of which are hard to give all of the time, so we must try harder. I liked how he told us to just make notes of the scriptures he would read from and refer to them later. This way we can listen to his message instead of turning pages the whole time.

Then I guess the fishermen I saw came to hear his message, "Go Deep!" He reminded us once again about going deep into our works of faith. Proverbs 16:3, "Commit your works to the Lord." Everybody can do something and that's all you have to do. When you know Jesus and you're able to do more, then you will do more. First of course you have to take care of yourself. Your weaknesses and pains can make you stronger if you recognize the mighty power that heals you daily. Matthew 5:16 says: "Let your light shine so that everyone can see your good works." Put "your house" in order and also take time to help your neighbors while you are working on "your house." There will always be more to do. We must be steady in our daily work so that we'll be able to adjust if something more important is needed.

I was surprised after listening to the dance theme on the radio on the drive out that the sermon started out mentioning dancing. Jesus was exalted and the angels were twirling. Mention of more dancing can be found in Psalm 30:11. David danced in 2 Samuel 6. The children danced in Job 21:11 and Psalm 149:3. Also a beautiful song back in the 60's mentions dancing and is from Ecclesiastes 3. Bad dances in Exodus 32:19 and Matthew 14:6—then sad dances in Lamentations 5:15. All of this leads us to the end of "our dance" on Earth and our possibility of an encore in heaven.

Ch 48

WOW! This week's church was very energetic! The worship room was small because it was in an old store, but it felt like I was going to see a music gig because they had a full band. The early service was leaving as I was getting there so that also gave it a busy and exciting feeling. I had also seen this church on the way to "the city." It's in the next town south of us and is in their downtown. I planned this church today since it is a little closer and I could get back for the start of this week's NASCAR race. I have to listen to the beginning of the race so I can concentrate on writing this. This church was a Christian grace church and by coincidence my Daily Reader this morning was about "grace"—Ephesians 2:8. I liked their Sunday morning bulletins which were larger than most churches and had a place on the back for notes. I liked having the children in the service but some of the parents couldn't listen to the sermon for disciplining their kids. The kids need a church that is so much fun that when they go to school, they tell all of the other kids about it.

I had read in my newspaper this morning—in the Religious Section—an article on *fear*, and I was surprised that the first thing the preacher mentioned in his topic of the day was about fear. He said that unfaithful fear is no match for faithful strength. We fear losing our jobs and losing all of our stuff. This is called "anxious" fear which is different from the more obvious types of fear. Don't fear anyone who is different. Your fear should be reserved only for things that could hurt your family. If you hate or fear a person, you are wasting your energy that could be used to improve your life. There's also real fear which you don't have much control over like prison and war. When you find yourself in one of these situations, all other fear seems minor. When you lose control over your own life, you will feel real fear—fear that you might not live long enough to get another chance at life.

In the Bible, Isaiah 61 proclaims the opening of your own personal prison.

Don't be surprised when you offend somebody or even get arrested. It happens "all of the time." This should be a time for you to reflect and reevaluate your actions. Many adults feel that whatever they are doing is OK because they are the provider for the family or they run the household. Many times adults can be abrupt and "set in their ways." They do not listen to the family enough to actually consider anything that the rest of the family may be feeling. You should take some time off from whatever you regularly do so you can objectively consider your actions and consider an alternative way of life. Many times you will already know what you are doing is wrong, but you are so used to your habits that you automatically do them. Easy change is usually a change for the worse. Forced change will make you a better person.

You'll never get life figured out but a few successes will overcome many failures so you must keep trying. Your project becomes easy when you set your mind to it. In the old days, people had to work together in order to build many things which, today, are built by machines. But by working together, they were able to build many things. The downside of all this "working together" is that they were forced to work together by their kings. When a man is given too much power, it often leads to war. So watch your leaders, work on your projects, organize all big jobs with others, and understand the different types of fear.

Ch 49

This Sunday, I planned on a little trip back to where it all began. Well at least where it all began after life in the big city. I moved to this county and "by the lake" about 15 years ago to get away from the fast life.

The church today is in that same little bitty town where I had a rent house for four years before I bought a house with a shop. My mom's house, my house, and this church are all in the same county but about 20 miles apart.

The "big" city might have had more bars, a lot more, but in the country, it's easier to make dope. As the old saying goes, "I went out of the frying pan and into the fire." I bought and sold dope to my "friends" and we were seldom bored. It was one big long party—about a decade's worth. The city was a rat race but the dope game is even worse. You're always looking for someone—going, going, going! We drank beer instead of water. When we got too drunk, we'd do more speed. And in between, we'd smoke a little weed to make it all feel better.

Anyway, the neighborhood where this church is located made me think about all of that, and I didn't stay for the whole church service. I don't know if it wasn't as exciting as some of the other churches I've been to lately, or if it was just how the area made me feel. I was going to go by the house across the street from where I used to live, but the last time I heard, dope was there.

So I turned the other way and stopped by a guy's house that used to be my best friend before I got on the needle. My old friend was a dairy farmer and I figured they would be at church, but I wanted to at least leave them a business card while I was in the neighborhood. They used to go to church in the same town as another type of church I visited, but I went by there on that trip and that church had moved. They wrote me the last time I got locked up but not this time. None of your "friends" write when you get locked up—at least not for long. So I haven't been in a rush to find any of my old "friends."

When I left their house, I took a different way home. The way that leads to that curvy road I told you about in Ch 34. Driving these roads brings back lots of old memories. I passed the houses of several people who are now in prison. Then I remembered "the little girl" lived on this road. I thought for a second that she might be playing in the yard. I've never seen her and I often wonder if she really is my daughter. Well as I drove by, there she was … standing at the front door holding the screen open like she was looking for me.

I've been staying to myself a lot since I've been out of prison. I don't want to go back. Prison is REALLY, REALLY BORING!

What if the things you were doing were judged wrong? Would you want forgiveness? The Lord looks to see if there are any who understand this. Those who know of their sin look happy and their punishment comes from within. Your fury would only feed their fire and increase their strength. To cure a problem, you must first cure your hate and not bear this sin against your brother.

Ch 50

Like the rock band Europe sang, "It's the final countdown!" I'm in the fifties now with only two more churches to go! Mom and I drove over a hundred miles back to the real big city where we were both born and raised. What a beautiful day for the first day of April! Today's church was in an office complex and it was the most modern church so far. The free coffee, doughnuts, and cookies might have been my favorite part!

This was a spiritual-living type of church and it was a little different from any other church I've been to. They had great music and even had a Grand Piano! The lead guitar player woke everybody up! I never heard one word about Jesus or that is was Palm Sunday. It was more of a contemporary church like Ch 17. There were guys there but it seemed like a "chick" church to me. It definitely smelled good, but I think part of it was from the perfume of the cute lady who sat right in front of me. They had tissues everywhere for several crying women. The pastor was a lady and she reminded me of the lady pastor in Ch 35. I had to stop writing and go check my files to make sure they had different names; they do! I really liked the pastor in Ch 35, and I didn't get to talk to the pastor today, but she looked like a lot of fun. In the Big City, people don't greet you as much as they do in the country, but if you locked eyes with someone long enough, they would say, "Hi." They did have a special time where everyone met the people sitting by them.

They follow some of the "science" philosophies that were made famous by Mary Baker Eddy, and when they acknowledged Emma Curtis Hopkins, it took me awhile but I finally figured out I had those two mixed up. Emma was a student of Mary's, and she had a "new thought" movement back when women weren't leaders like they are now. Emma was determined to be happy and she wasn't going to let anything get in her way. Later she taught many others to minister in her unique style.

It was the week that they celebrated new members and each new member was assigned a "pal." Their "pal" will be available to them for any problems they need spiritual help with. They all sat on the first two rows. Their "pals" lit candles and stood up on the first step of the stage in front of them. The new members then stood in front of their "pal" as they were passed candles. The candles represent life—life which all of us share.

This church was so modern. The kids took the elevator up to the second floor where they have church. Our service was very different from the mainstream, and I wondered what the young people were being taught. At the end of the service, the children came down and stood on the stage. There were almost as many kids at this church as there were adults! Happy kids make happy churches and happy churches make happy families.

Ch 51

Well yesterday was Good Friday. I don't know why they call it that. Maybe it's because all of the kids get out of school! And a lot of people get off work! I'll check into that. But tonight we are going to the city for Church #51 in this book. Sometimes I worry about running out of topics to write about. So, when I saw this event advertised in the newspaper, I decided this church would be a good one for the second to the last church in this book.

Tomorrow is Easter and I will be going back to the church where I got baptized last year on Easter. Since I've already included that church in this book, we are driving about 40 miles to the closest city tonight so I will have another new church this week. The church right across the street in our town is the same kind, but they haven't been open lately. I tried to go to it in Ch 25. I sure thought that church would make the book and it's strange how the closest church to me didn't make one of the 52. Well I guess in an ironic way, they will! I'll tell you all about it in the morning.

Now it's Sunday afternoon and I just got back from church. First I'll tell you about the big show we saw last night. They had live animals and a cast of what looked like over a hundred people. The horse they had was as beautiful an animal as I've ever seen. And the camel was—well a camel! We don't see too many of those around here. There was also a donkey and some lambs. The play was about the crucifixion of Jesus Christ by the Romans and his disappearance from the tomb—or as many believe, his resurrection. One of the many versions of the Bible says that when we are resurrected, we will be like angels of God—but only those who have done mostly good deeds. Those who died still doing evil will be condemned for each evil deed.

There is no doubt that Jesus was a very good Jewish preacher and it is uncanny how there are no reports of his doing any bad deeds. Some believe he was a prophet and some believe he was the son of God. Centuries before Jesus of Nazareth, many people believed in the resurrection or the "dying-and-rising" theory of several earthbound gods where their souls will continue to live after their body dies. Many people believe that a resurrection is when you face God on your "Judgment Day" and that our beliefs will determine the path that our souls will take after our body dies. Some believe that our soul will be in "limbo" by some of the many electronic forces that scientists are still discovering—and that they are held somewhere out in the universe and will be judged at the same time someday. Some call this the "End Times" but it is hard to imagine the actual end of time. It seems that *something* will always exist!

Ch 52

Today we will drive back to the Real Big City and finish up this book with what I like to call the "movie star" religion. A lot of people idolize musicians and movie stars so I thought I'd let this be the "Grand Finale" of my book. Maybe some musicians and movie stars will read this book and realize how lucky they are to be in the positions that they are in. Maybe then the ones who think they are better than everyone else will realize that it's only a gift that they have been given. Maybe then all entertainers will start to act in a manner that allows not only young people, but also parents to be proud of them.

This facility was in an old million-dollar mansion. As we walked through the "house," I could imagine the family that used to live there with kids running and playing up and down the stairs and it also made me wonder what they are doing now that they have grown up. The actual service though was real disappointing. The first speaker went into too much detail and tried to cover too much material too fast. This church was founded by a famous author and promoter and some of the material is too deep or complicated to be read as quickly as the speaker was reading. Then the next speaker wanted you to focus on the wall, and then the chair, and then the floor, and he repeated these steps too many times for new visitors.

This place looked like a library or a book store with all of the esoteric, philosophical teaching material. Some of the books teach you about things—like how important personal integrity is and not to look just at what we see but to observe what we see.

They believe that all races are equal and should be able to practice any religion and that all men have the right to be able to talk freely and write freely and support whatever group they want. Now they may say they believe all of this but we all know that somewhere there is a line that can't be crossed. They work towards the goal of ending war and poverty on our planet. I also believe that when everyone really wants this to happen that it will be possible. One of my future projects, I hope, will be to organize people into specific topics that I think are very important. These problem areas are so vast that the only way they can be cured is by the organization of a lot of people who can work together towards the same goal. They also believe, like I do, that the Justice System is dangerously flawed and its punishment structure needs to be modernized. I don't like non-prisoners or non-drug-addicts talking about prisoners and drug addicts because they just don't know. The speaker said that no prisoner will admit that he was wrong and that is just not true!

They have people working in what they call divisions to promote the material they sell and they seem to have some very worthwhile projects, including helping people get off dope. And since that was the main purpose of this book, I changed my mind about their program at the end. Now I think I may visit their new $3 million facility they are building in the fancy neighborhood where I used to cruise around in my hot-rods and trucks when I was a young man!

CLOSING

Well I could have written more about many of the subjects in this book. But I wrote it so it could be read slowly enough for your thoughts to sink in, while at the same time be completed and quickly loaned to someone else who can benefit from my experiences.

This is my last chance to give you anymore information. Religion and politics bring out the best and worst in people—but they both "have to be done." What if you bought a used car and then one day you got pulled over for speeding and the police dog found some hidden dope. You would be guilty until proven innocent, and you might spend a long time in jail. Only religion and politics working together can solve such a problem.

The Bible is a good book to read! While I was in prison, I finally read it cover to cover and very slowly so it could sink in. I have several versions of it and I enjoy the easy-to-read versions with a lot of references and possible meanings of some of the old text. I still have to read the other popular religious books and now that I'm through writing this book maybe I can.

Some of the Old Testament is weird sounding and really hard to understand—like Leviticus with all of the sacrifices and laws about what to eat. Some of my favorite parts of the Bible are in what's called the "Wisdom Books." One of the oldest stories is about Job and his sufferings and his reward. I really like Proverbs with its life-guiding principles which can still be used today. All through the Bible you'll find parts in it that are your favorites. While you are reading it or reading it again, you can make notes of your favorite parts so that when you have finished, you can go back and read those parts over and over.

When you feel like you shouldn't do something, people call that your conscience. "Con" is to learn or teach a lesson and "science" is knowledge. So your conscience is God's experiment to see if we will listen.

I love all of the new online church vessels for people, mostly young people, to find and consider a legal way to find happiness. I hope that they can get together with the other young people in their area and find a church that allows them to form the churches of the future. If you undermine the members of your group, no matter how different or bad they are, how can you expect anyone to join your group? When you wonder why your group is a failure, it just might be because of you!

INCARNATE: To put in human form – INCARCERATE: To put in prison

When you are incarcerated, you awake from your good dreams of being free or even your bad dreams to an even worse reality. You must endure your burden of sin which placed you there. Your mind flexes and you bend every thought to avoid the point that would cause you to break. When I was in prison, one of my favorite sayings was, "all things will pass." Well I guess I'm talking about the bad things—because I hope the good things stick around forever!

Sometimes I think if I had more money, I could have spent more time on this book. But the truth is if I had had more money, I probably would have been out doing other things, and I would not have slowed down long enough to write it. If any aspects of my life would have been different, this book would be different. It would be way different, like not written at all.

So we ended up with what we have—a book written by a guy during the first year he got out of prison and it's just as imperfect as we all are.

WORK LIKE YOU ENJOY IT

LOVE LIKE YOU HAVE NEVER BEEN HURT

DANCE LIKE NOBODY'S WATCHING

Made in the USA
Monee, IL
04 November 2026

67385473R00089